Driftwood Holly

THE ART OF BEING MYSELF

MY LIFE JOURNEY FROM BEHIND THE IRON
CURTAIN INTO THE WILDERNESS OF THE YOKON

Bibliographic information from the German National Library: The German National Library lists this publication in the German National Bibliography; Detailed bibliographic data is available on the Internet at http://dnb.dnb.de.

© 2025 Driftwood Holly

Proofreading: Annemoon Mater
Layout: Mirko Dominiak
Coverdesign: Dr. Dazey
Contributors: Dana Earthchild, Kiki, Mette Glargaard, and my parents
Verlag: BoD · Books on Demand GmbH, In de Tarpen 42, 22848 Norderstedt, bod@bod.de
Druck: Libri Plureos GmbH, Friedensallee 273, 22763 Hamburg

ISBN: 978-3-7693-4973-3

Inhaltsverzeichnis

Photo by Jürgen Ihle

Many thanks to all the diligent helpers of this book's creation.

You are an integral part of everything I am. Cheers to Dana Earthchild, Kiki, Mette Glargaard, Dr. Dazey, Annemoon Mater, Mirko Dominiak and my parents.

INTRO

Here it is, my first book. And once again, I'm doing it the way I like to approach my new adventures: diving in and learning how to swim. This book is me, or more so, who I once was. Not a philosophical guide to live by, but rather a bird's-eye view of myself. It will lovingly tell you everything that has happened to me and how I decided at the many crossroads of life's pathways. I warmly invite you to have your own adventure with my story. And it's quite a wild tale that I want to tell you while sitting here in front of my blazing fireplace, warming my knees. Outside, in the wilderness, it's -37 degrees today, giving the Yukon winter its unique beauty and turning it into a land that forgives almost nothing.

My book will take you roughly up to my 30th year and took more than 15 years. The richness of events and experiences has not diminished thereafter, so this Holly Life simply couldn't be put into a single book.

During the initial stage of my journey, I felt the impact of past generations and the effect of their choices. Yet, it also reveals how my unconventional and sometimes mischievous ways of thinking shaped my own path and the situations I encountered. This led to both favorable outcomes and moments of complete chaos.

It certainly was never boring. I have a wonderful life, and the fact that I get to experience all this, surprises even a lifelong adventurer like me very much.

Our unique world often changes faster than we can perceive it, and we are required to make decisions that we do not seem to be capable of in the moment. Trust that everything is in flux is only gained over time.

Now you can wander joyfully through my little book, find things that resonate with you, and maybe it opens your heart to new ways you haven't walked yet. Maybe it gives you courage for a step you always wanted to take. But mostly I hope you can laugh as childishly as I did while writing this. The whole drama of a boy who wanted to learn to fly but landed in the trenches between two world powers and was ultimately swept into the real wilderness by the flow of life.

I wish you a beautiful journey and sincerely hope that reading my book enriches your life.

Driftwood Holly

HOME

The art of being myself… begins in Oberwiesenthal, a small energy place in Saxony's Ore Mountains of Germany, where peculiar characters have settled for centuries.

I was born in Zwickau, but immediately transported to my new home. By my grandpa, in a Trabant. My daddy Heri had already gone ahead and so it remained the task of my grandfather to dig little Holly through the Winter Wonderland to the top of the highest mountain in the country. The 'carton de la Papp' (yes, we had a car out of pressed cardboard in the GDR) had no 4 wheel drive and needed real drivers. I don't remember this trip of course, but when I get stuck in the Yukon winter with my little ones today, I can literally taste the atmosphere in the Trabi when the word „responsibility" takes on a completely different meaning. If you were stuck in the old days, nobody came. Just like the Yukon wilderness. You have to get „unfucked" by yourself.

The resort town and wintersport center of our country was located on the socialist Fichtelmountain at 3982 feet. After traveling to 40 countries and thousands of places during my life, I can say now, there was hardly a better place to be a kid. And I am still that kid today. A childish man who never gets tired of looking behind every curtain. The peace that socialism harbored gave us unrestricted freedom of movement, unnoticed by us at the time, of course. My parents had good work, the village cop was not the brightest and always too slow. And there was something very abundant: children. The streets were safe and full of them, an unbelievable wealth from today's perspective. Nobody could shoot you out of the street game with a mouse click. There was still real laughter, shoving, stealing, hiding, and when mom called you home by screaming your name out of the window, you were deaf. One rather took the furious Mother than to miss even one act of this street carnival. Television was limited to DDR1 and DDR2 and only emptied the streets on Sundays at 2 pm when Professor Flimmrich showed one of the DEFA films. The films of the GDR are still strange but so wonderful today.

I always had heroes in my life, not too many but I felt comfortable around some characters and there was a kind of energy exchange, which of course could be dismissed as friendship. But if I look back from today, I can say that between us there was a closeness that was more like a little love.

My mother could never stand one of them. But that's how love is... Jens, called „the bull", was much older than me and came from a family that wasn't really one. I was, I think, the first who really listened to him and I found he knew so much more than all the others who, because of my smallishness, preferred to knock me down the slope rather than play with me. He was tall and an excellent bodyguard with wiry strength to pick the locks that remained closed to me. I enjoyed him and he was happy to teach me and be a friend.

My second hero was my ski jumping coach Joachim Loos. An old man, from a children's perspective, who was able to charm you, always, with amazement. He was the first magician in my life. A romantic who created atmospheres in which people talked with hand puppets or marveled at his mini spruces, which he had planted between his double window. He had invented „skiing in the summer". It went wonderfully on a special grass with short skis, polished with shoeshine. We were proud as knights when we went to this secret hillside in the height of summer and googly eyed tourists asked us, „Where do you want to go with those skis in this weather?" „Skiing, stupid!" and on we went, laughing like children, convinced that we would get a good head start for the season because we knew „Mr. Loos".

He took 20 pfennigs from us for every bad word that left our mouth and gave it back to us as cookies and cocoa for the Christmas party. And in my opinion, he is responsible for the development of most of the imitation equipment in German ski jumping that is still used today. A wonderful person who always believed in Holly as a person, despite my initial slim athletic performance. And there were not many of them who did bother to help me because I was loud, flimsy and maybe a bit annoying? I kept visiting him later in life, like many other GDR athletes who trained with him. This was the compliment for Achim, which he had never received from sports officials. He was simply different, he was alive, searching and finding. There was hardly a moment that was not special next to him and even when he scolded you, you felt respected. He was the first really different person and so much more alive than all the other „straighteners".

Thank you Achim, also on behalf of all the others who never had the chance to say that.

Oberwiesenthal

Holly and mom

WAITING AT THE WINDOW

Oberwiesenthal probably also invented Christmas, and even today, many years after the fall of communism, only one cheap blinking plastic fairy light has made it to the land of candles and wood carvers. Did you know that Santa Claus was green until a caffeinated drink in a red can was marketed?

The winter time had always transformed the small town into a fairytale. Probably the most intense memory of this time was waiting for my dad. At that time, he was a physiotherapist for the Olympic winter sports team and disappeared with the colorful leaves in the fall, reappearing with the spring birds. Every now and then, he came from the mystical world that was very distant to me for many years to get the laundry done, make mom happy, and bring me a little gift from „The West". I sat on the wide window frame in the kitchen, the one where he would first appear. It was always dark, and mom and I had made it all cozy, with enough macaroni, incense charming the room, and blankets to wrap ourselves up in. And then we waited there.

Across the street was a lantern, fat snowflakes floating in its light cone. We kept looking at each other, and there was so much tension that these moments are still burned into my kids' brain. And then he came out of the dark. Mostly dragging heavy bags and making the first new tracks through the snow. He appeared like a Santa Claus that always liked me, then again mom didn't tell him everything I had done...

I usually offered to help him unpack right in the hallway to get my gift faster. He never made me wait long, and I happily went to bed with my new toy so he could take care of mom and make sure my sister would get born.

I think this story belongs here because I really enjoy telling it. The loving closeness to my mother during this time and the excitement and joy when my father came home have become truly vivid childhood memories. Until I was 18, I tried to become the ski jumping world champion at the sports school. My father suggested that I become a Nordic combined athlete, a mixed event of ski jumping and cross-country skiing, because there were fewer competitors, given my not-so-great talent. So I did.

These 12 years of GDR competitive sport were very, very full, and it was a time in which I could do almost anything with my body. I wasn't really that good, but I belonged to a club that hosted incredible talent. The GDR was somehow great for sport. The worst thing about my sports career was that my dad worked at the same club. Every one of my trainers, teachers, and educators quickly found their way to him to complain about my unruliness. None of the other children had their parents close so I always had to pay twice for every misbehavior.

During this formative time, I discovered the sweetness of „the girls", who completely distracted me from my plans to become world champion. Oh dear, can you imagine what goes on in a boarding school with 300 young pubescents? Now honestly, would you have focused on getting constantly exhausted from sport or would you try to hang out with the crowning glory of creation?

But there was an army of guards standing in the way of all this fun. We were not allowed in their rooms, and there was a strict separation between the genders. It was very hard to sneak into a dark corner of a TV room and steal a kiss. And so it happened that I was caught practicing my first French kiss in the hallway, but not with a girl! No, with my buddy. Yes, it always started with the boys. I can still laugh heartily today that we preferred to educate each other because we still just froze in the presence of a princess. But from then on, I was constantly in love with one or more of these young women who didn't just look like goddesses in their race outfits, but also liked me more than the boys ever did. Being with them was way more harmonious and fulfilling for me. That never changed in my life until today; you will find me with the females.

By the way, I didn't become a world champion. I was fired for not listening and just not having it in me to go all the way to the top like some of my buddies did. And to the top they went, and they made sports history. I was lucky to be a part of this.

Me and my dad

ALMOST CHAMPION

The greatest gift of competitive sports, aside from free trips to the Eastern Bloc, eating tropical fruits in winter, and having access to the best sports equipment, is the awareness of one's own body. You can move so skillfully, know your limits, constantly push them, and develop a very intimate relationship with your own body. This is a significant reason why, despite some doubts about the competitive sports system, I still consider it a valuable form of youth development. I put in a lot of effort to become something more, but I simply didn't have what it takes. And „learning to fly" next to Jens Weißflog, Matti Nykänen, and Andi Goldberger was not all that enjoyable. It was more like a car race against Ayrton Senna.

However, I did become the German 'almost champion' in Nordic Combined, and not winning the title was just as dramatic as it sounds. On competition days, we were usually served a nice meal in one of the local restaurants. We enjoyed wild meat with red cabbage and dumplings. I usually felt awful on those days, tortured with a form of stage fright, and could hardly keep the food down. We had to hike a steep hill of about two kilometers to reach the ski jump. Surprisingly, I felt quite at ease, while usually, during this phase, I would experience my first signs of weakness. But this time, the ascent was smooth, and I soon found out why, still being under the impression I was in good shape.

So, we arrived at the ski jump on top of the mountain, and before we began our very individual and often spiritual warm-up, I took a close look at the 'hill'.
You talk to the ski jump and believe that if you estab-
lish some warm connection with it, it will launch you
far down into the valley and keep you safe at the
same time in this insane endeavor. So, I started with
my self-motivating ritual and meditation mix. Everyone was watching each other. What wax were others
using? Did they talk to one another? And where's the
balance between warming up and getting fatigued? In
between, swallow the dumpling again and just
breathe. At some point, it was time to change into
our ski jumping equipment. We usually had our suits
already on, but not the gloves, helmets, and jumping
boots, which were like elephant feet. So, I grabbed
my backpack...

„Wait, which backpack? Oh, no, I left it in the restaurant!" The thoughts racing through my mind at that
moment were beyond belief. The situation just could-
n't be real. This was the highlight of the competition
year, and I was without my gear. Time seemed to
stand still. I was in a daze as I made my way to my
coach. „I left my ski jumping gear in the pub!", I said.
He just took a long look at me, probably thinking,
„You probably won't win anyway...", then came his
calm response: ¡What should I do about it now?" I
was frozen and felt dead.

Slowly, this rigor mortis turned into action – and
what action it was. I raced down the hill like someone
running for their life. My mediocrity had granted me
a pair of worn-out sneakers that were now paying

off. I slid down that two-kilometer slope at full speed without even considering the possibility of a fall. I hit the wall of the restaurant with my windblown frozen hair, grabbed my backpack, and went back. A Wartburg car (for those unfamiliar, a mid-range East German car) happened to pass by, billowing two-stroke smoke. „I need to get up the hill", I said, and the panic in my eyes probably made the driver think of something more serious than just an East German championship. He stammered: „Okay" and I was already in the car. „Thank you." Off we went.

Where no car had ventured before, this savior now attempted to climb this hill. Stopping was not an option. Somewhere on the way, the force of gravity and the snow brought us to a halt. I was relieved when the car stuck to the incline, and hanging on the door, I whispered: „Thank you."

I never found out how he got back down, and if you were the driver and recognize this story, please contact me. You drove an „almost champion"!

So, onward. This time, the rest of the uphill race was a bit more challenging because I had all my gear with me. I ran until I was out of breath, and I could hear the start numbers announced over the loudspeakers at the ski jump, getting closer and closer to my number. Upon reaching the top, I hastily put on my gear, grabbed my skis, and sprinted up the tower. I had already been announced, but at this point, everyone could see me. My coach lowered his head, and they gave me a few bonus seconds... Strap on the skis and go. I was in the track, racing at breakneck speed down the inrun towards the takeoff. The jump that followed was more like an attempt to catch my breath. I flew, laid back, exhausted, in the air carried by my skis, and flew far. Bang! Sensation!

Leading after the first round. Back then there were no lifts, and we walked up the hill, and halfway there, at the judges' tower, I met my coach. I had the eyes of a leader, and then he said, „Well, you're finally for once properly warmed up". This sentence has also remained a lasting memory. I can laugh about it now, but back then, it pierced my heart. I then finished second after the ski jumping, with a relatively small gap behind the first-place athlete and me.

Back then, under the „Gundersen method", the first to cross the finish line in the cross-country race would win the overall event. My coach's affection for me was now boundless. I was the inferior cross-country skier, and I felt sick, chased, ready for defeat. Still, I set off with the goal of not being overtaken and earning a medal. This was my chance to go to the youth competitions in the Soviet Union and secure my place in the A-Team. I could see the competitor who started behind me in his Dynamo Klingenthal racing suit, and I ran without any strategy. And he stuck with me, as if in a dream, one where you can't escape no matter how hard you try. Almost at the same moment that the one behind me gasped for breath, the leader in front of me appeared, his running style falling apart. What was happening? Here I was, with the opportunity to turn the tables. The coach yelled, „He's done. He's done!"

Just one kilometer downhill to go, and then the final sprint.

I overtook him up the hill, but his skis were faster on the downhill, and I ended up in second place again. Another two hundred meters, and he was crying. I pushed myself to catch up, swerved in the finishing area, and briefly took the lead. Then, just as I was about to win, an unexpected twig from the course marking got caught in my binding and wouldn't let go. I hobbled with that darn thing to the finish line and won my first watch with just two meters behind a very likable champion. Years later, I learned that this same young man got testicular cancer, just like me. The second intense experience we shared. This time around, we both became champions.

Learning to fly

Running for my life

LOVING THE GIRLS

So I grew up, clashed with authorities, and lost my innocence at the age of 13.9, but I continued to focus on life. Even back then, I realized that I couldn't relate much to the habits of the 'mainstream youth'. However, I never felt like I was just against something as a principle. Instead, many behavioral patterns and communications of the crowd felt a bit empty or at least strange. It often seemed like I was a know-it-all, questioning why 'they' all did the same thing. The physically taller and considerably stronger people of my age and the authorities with plenty of long-arm power could easily push me aside or label me as foolish, which I suffered greatly from. I was basically powerless and bullied for all those years. During that time, the feeling arose that while they could effectively silence me, my own truth didn't disappear from within me. But I admit that it was often very amusing to challenge them or to drive my fellow human's crazy until their glasses fogged up from the inside.

It's very pleasant that today, many of these people remember me and are happy to see me, and I believe that this is a genuine feeling. We've lived a piece of life together, and it was always exciting because I wanted to discover new things, and the normal routine was simply boring. The worst was probably when they had to laugh but couldn't or didn't want to. I gladly took on the laughter. Yes, I was a shit disturber. But it was good shit.

The first people I really felt comfortable with were the girls. Not just sexually curious, but with the premonition that there was more to discover, I slowly ventured forward into this new world. What was truly wonderful about these sweet women was that they could understand me. They liked to listen to the little adventure stories and enjoyed the closeness and laughter I could produce. I was delighted to finally be greeted with a smile when I showed up and kind of got addicted to making them feel good or to trigger their imagination. I was bathing in this new warm pool full of life and beauty, and I made sure my daily paths would cross as much as possible. They didn't keep telling everyone how smart they were. They were simply smarter and still are today. I have great admiration for the clarity and wisdom of women to this day and would like to apologize to those whose hearts I wounded in my quest for my dream woman.

Even today when I'm in a bar or wherever people gather, I prefer to sit at the women's table. My life has become so much more beautiful since you appeared in my emotional world. There are many enriching experiences from this time of blossoming and finding one's way. Today I know that every interaction had a smaller or larger effect on me. But it takes a whole lifetime to somewhat organize your books in this unique 'library of love' for everyone. There are hardly any shortcuts to find in this field. It's about discovering who we really are and what misconceptions or inherited behavioral patterns we have been exposed to. The stuff that didn't help was mostly well disguised and hard to let go of.

To be weak as a man was simply impossible and very out of fashion when I was young. While women were somehow always considered weaker or not as capable, men ruled with a kind of 'universal approval,' not only causing all the wars, discrimination, and a lot of pain, but also fueling the exhausting competition of bullying. Of course, there were exceptions in the man's world, but they were not loud and had to be very strong to hold their ground. The male friendships in my life, from back then and today, are all friends who also have a soft, forgiving side. In my experience, companionship, pleasure, or work proved to be way more fruitful and long-lasting with women or „not-so-tough" men.

I truly believe that if the world were ruled by mothers, there would be no more wars because no one would go to them anymore, and secondly, men could finally do what they're really good at: fishing and bullshitting.

HERTA AND WAG

During this same time, I also had very pleasant friends on my side. In life, people often ask the question of how many good friends one has and say that one should be grateful if there are at least two. I believe that this cliché has no justification for its existence. In my life, there are only very few friends for a lifetime. There are actually a lot of friends for a specific period. They always appear at the right time and are always the best cast. This never excluded staying connected, but the 'high-time' was always related to a specific phase of life. I am very happy that it is this way because it allows me to look forward to very close and heartfelt connections in the future with friends, I don't even know yet. Everyone in this circle brings something that is absolutely indispensable for further development.

During this time, my friend was „Herta". A few years older and an absolute spur-of-the-moment decision maker. Herta was a born tramp who knew a thousand jokes and songs, and he would immediately take a seat at the regulars' table in every pub, making everyone there feel like they had been waiting just for him. And he was wonderfully gentle. We had probably the most romantic trips together. Large hats, fringed jackets, fringed boots – all self-assembled due to the lack of stuff in our country, and therefore very valuable. In his father's house, there were so many signs with instructions, that if you ever needed to go to the bathroom, you had pissed yourself before you read it all. Do I need to mention that his parents didn't like me very much because they thought I led their son into strange things? Well, little did they know about their own son, and nothing was strange about us, in my opinion.

Every Friday, after the pub closed around 2 am, we would stumble to the narrow-gauge railroad station and stoke the stove in the conductor's car. There, we would sit and dream about everything that Tom Sawyer and Huck Finn had left for us to discover. Then, at 4:55 am, the conductor would come and get that train in motion. Lots of steam, lots of puffing, very little motion. First, he was a bit irritated by us being there but after a few times, he had gotten used to us and the already warm stove. After about an hour of riding with this beautiful steaming locomotive into the sunrise, we arrived at a bakery, got off, and shared our very important knowledge with the people waiting in line. Then we got fresh, crusty buns with butter and a coffee, jumped on the next train back, climbed on top of the roof of the last car and devoured our breakfast riding back up to our mountain town. The special effect of a hard working steam engine made this quite the fairy tale. It was just too good not to do it, this was true adventure.

Herta taught me to see interesting things and that our rules were just as good as anybody's. The golden rule was always not to hurt or scare anyone. We saw ourselves more as the „good vibe boys". Herta never gave up this party life and is now an angel by his own choice. My thoughts on his death? Well... that's very delicate ground, and I won't dance on it. I got to feel the full extent of his soft heart. Others who he would have loved to show it to, missed out big time on that privilege. See you soon, my good friend... I know where to find you, Maestro.

The other person from that time, and still a dear friend, is „dor Wag". To this day, I'm not sure whether the sports management had chosen him to keep me a bit under control. He was a successful Nordic combined skier with a junior world championship title, and I still don't know exactly what brought us together back then. He was not a rebel at all. He was more like, steady girlfriend, riding motorcycles slowly, and just generally being nice. A fine fellow, really. If I try to grasp what it was at this moment, I think it was his humor and intelligence. Yes, he was sharp in the mind, and I wanted to know everything about him. We became inseparable and developed our own language that often had us laughing our heads off. Yes, it was the laughter. Endlessly long silly conversations. We could have filled ten absolutely useless books.

There was a time when our brains were working in synchronicity and we spoke in harmony. We had even worked out a special nod that told the one nodded at: „You say it". Yes, it was the fun that connected us, and so it happened that Wag enjoyed my little irregularities beside the sport more and more. And I felt great because the sports authorities always thought that when I was with him, everything would be under control. No... it went wild! And so, increasingly often, we found ourselves sitting in front of the colorful woven tapestry of the club boss office for discussions about our escapades. „We really didn't know" was the phrase that always got you off the hook, because it was a sort of confession and included a youthful innocence, all the while keeping the hope alive that we would start 'thinking' soon. And we had already started and wanted to quit the high-performance sport. We weren't going to become world champions anyway, and the rest was gradually becoming very strenuous. But it wasn't that simple. The real world was waiting with jobs, of which we knew very little about. The world outside of sports looked pretty scary but we needed to go there. But the leadership didn't accept our applications to quit. The state had invested so much and told us we had to keep going for the republic. So, we decided to keep making mistakes, and after a good week of this carnival, I was dishonorably discharged, and Wag was being let go for 'health reasons' due to his good reputation. We never lost sight of each other, and when we occasionally meet, the goofiness is as fresh as in the good old days and so... „The good old days are today.

Herta and me

Wag with milk

UNCLE NEIL YOUNG

My friend Wag also summoned another person into my life who has not left me to this day. I feel sorry for all the generations of humanity that had to do without him. Ladies and gentlemen, my deepest gratitude to......Neil Young.

Yes, even now, I have tears in my eyes. This philosophical songwriter and -poet has played the soundtrack to my life and is not finished yet. No matter what happens in your life, Uncle Neil has a song that helps you understand it. A song that makes you feel free when you're walking down the highway. Or one to close your eyes to while you rock out all your frustration on the dance floor in unrestrained wildness. He writes melodies that can make your experiences explode or in certain situations simply put you in a state of suspension, like life's doping. Neil is a messenger who leads you to yourself and asks you uncompromising questions.

Being about 25 years older than me, he also gives me the advantage of having experienced a lot and, when I need information for myself, his songs swing it into my consciousness pre-digested.

After my immigration to Canada, I began to understand the rest of the lyrics and became a musician myself. When I play music now, I get to enjoy this cocktail of enhanced emotions and artistic expression firsthand, but from him I learned not to guide the process. He gave me permission to simply let it unfold, to just be the channel, not the maker. Neil has brought so much enduring magic into my life that it feels like he raised me. As if he really is the good, wise uncle who has the magic potion and shows you all the cool stuff. The uncle who understands you like no other. I can wholeheartedly invite you to welcome his music into your life. When he enters your world, I promise you that there is a lot waiting for you, and you'll later wonder where you've been lingering all this time. And who would have ever thought that I would carve a microphone stand for Neil... that happened too.

I have been standing on the stages of this world for 15 years now. I stopped hiding behind Neil Young covers a long time ago and became more courageous in doing my own thing. But not an evening goes by when I step into the spotlight and he doesn't accompany me in some way or encourage and reassure me with the presence of his wonderful magic.

Thank you, Neil.

LEARNING A TRADE

The sports were now over, and I was 19 years young.

It seemed like I had to learn something real now. All the rules for clean living in competitive sports were gone, and eight hour workdays awaited. Including the commute by the express bus, my apprenticeship as a car mechanic turned into an 11-hour endeavor each day. Well, it seemed like everyone did it, so it must've been be okay. So, I entered the grand theater of a government owned 'bus and truck repair shop', in a collection of buildings cobbled together during the difficult years of East Germany. They housed 'specialized' garages for trucks, buses, and the indestructible superstar of the East German fleet, the B 1000 (a smaller very versatile truck).

During my apprenticeship, I had to go through all the different departments, and every one of those shops had its own little world with kings, jesters, thieves, and everything else it takes to play the whole show. I found myself subject to a hierarchy that I didn't quite understand at first, since the best or most experienced didn't always end up at the top. Often, it was the oldest or the one with a discreet but well-hidden marriage to the socialist party who held the highest position. Besides, everyone was really fed up with apprentices. So, now what?

Earning around 170 Marks a month wasn't a breakthrough, but it was quite nice considering that back in those days, you could be hammered drunk for a lot less than today. Well, anyway, there was no way around this and I just had to start this job. Perhaps you've also experienced the paralyzing feeling when you enter a new company in the morning for the first time, and no one knows you or pays attention to you and you don't know whose toes you will end up stepping on.

Eventually, someone would take pity on the newcomer and cautiously approach me with the look in their eyes that read, „please don't be a complete idiot". If this didn't seem the case and you could signal that you actually wanted to learn something, there was always a noticeable relief. And I actually genuinely wanted to learn. Tom, my fellow apprentice, and me, understood instantly that the only way into the warm coffee room was to do good, and to do so fast. This holy chamber was technically off-limits for us, but if we managed to please the respective masters with completed tasks and applied the department's lingo, we occasionally found ourselves invited into that sacred coffee room.

Our newly befriended masters often clashed in there with those who had identified us as apprentices. We were still unworthy, and soon we'd be in their departments, and then we'd see. The worst was when you accidentally sat in a spot that belonged to a king who was still seeking recognition. Accusations were loudly proclaimed, and you'd shrink away like a dog caught stealing. Eventually, you realized the whole game was a two-class system that was present in every aspect of our country. There were those who were dangerous, because of their close ties to the secret service or the government, and they could really mess up your life. And then there were those who were cunning and had the skills to lead an excellent life in the underworld of my country.

This second group was the tight network of experts in whatever field they were in, connected to everyone who had something valuable to offer. Plus, you couldn't be an asshole if you wanted to be a part of this black market high society. But if you got in, you could find everything, like good beer, Christmas ornaments, or very rare spare parts. This was the source. The truck drivers operated an undercover network of suppliers. And we repaired their trucks.

Now, you might think we had to do that anyway, but the trick was to do it in such a way that we slowly were able to do them a few favors and get them back on their beloved road. In return we would be rewarded with goodies that no-one could get. Truckers hated downtime. I thought I was learning to repair trucks, but instead I got some fine lessons in micromanaging the wheeling and dealing behind the curtains of my homeland.

Another amusing side effect of such workplaces was the language they developed, and to this day, I still laugh at words like 'rubber dog' and „knownothing".

I'll also never forget one reaction of a master that became a symbol of brilliant leadership for me. On Fridays, we had to clean up from noon onwards, and it was meticulously ensured that the „Foolies" as we were called, had everything spotlessly clean by 3 pm. By 4 pm, no one was around anymore (for those from West Germany, a master earned 900 Marks... would you have stayed any longer?). So, we stood in the workshops and waited for 3 pm. Waiting wasn't our strong suit. Tom and I discovered an air hose that could be fitted with an aluminum rivet, and when Tom turned on the valve, this bullet shot through the room at supersonic speed. We had just loaded it, and Tom pulled the trigger by opening the valve, just in the moment when the master entered the workshop.

He just stood there, hands resting on his hips, and looked at me and Tom, knowing something big was up. I had covered the end of the hose with my thumb and was hiding it behind my back. His trained eye always found something that wasn't done to his satisfaction. But no matter how much he looked around, he found nothing except the tension that seemed to radiate from our faces. And there was a definite tension emanating from the air hose, which was attempting to fire the rivet at full pressure. My thumb was slowly losing the game. The master's eyes wandered until they finally found a garbage bin whose lid was slightly lifted by its contents. He approached, and the bin had to open its mouth. The tension couldn't have been any higher, and Tom's cheeks, inflated with laughter, didn't help to keep this fucking hose under control behind me. The lid of the bin fell and as the master's tongue was about to give the order, a shot was fired. While a wild, air-spraying hose danced behind me, our cannonball hit the double light bar above the master's head... an explosion followed by a shower of glass and darkness. No one could connect the various events to make any sense. Not even Tom, who looked at me in the remaining light as if I had concealed the effect of our gun from him. The shower of glass grew quieter, and a deep silence fell. We looked at the master, who shook his head and then calmly said, „Such a full bin? And sweep again, please." Then he disappeared into the half-darkness. We burst into uncontrollable laughter, relieved that it was only the lamp we had eliminated.

Any other master would likely have yelled something in blind rage. But the good ones kept their composure. We were proud of him and always enjoyed working with him, even though he sometimes looked at us with a slightly tilted head, as if asking, „What happened back then, on that Friday at 3:30 pm?" In any case, one rivet has made its way into a book, and Tom never ratted me out.

VISIONS AND REALITY

A lifelong career in such a company was simply unimaginable. Just like in sports, it was difficult for me to work under authorities who weren't really authorities in my eyes, at least most of them. I had no problem in general listening to people and following them if they had a certain magic about them. But that was in short supply. So, I ended up following people who had internalized the absolutely killing phrase, „We've always done it this way". My wheels were spinning for life, and I found myself in a rather hopeless situation. Sooner or later, I would clash with these „bosses", and whoever wins that battle was written in my country's law of a dictatorship. The future looked very bleak, and my ideas were quite meager. Everywhere I looked, I saw a lot of endless repetition or highly questionable life styles.

I still wonder today where the art was in my life back then. Theater, music, and the entire world of entertainers were hidden from me. I did attend many music festivals, but it never occurred to me to just join the circus. But who was I? Who did I want to be? So my father sat down with me, and we looked over the great wide land of possibilities. Art was not a means of livelihood in my father's eyes, and at the time, I had nothing I could present, at least not without ending up with a black eye. So, art was out. If my father hadn't come to my rescue back then, I think I could have easily wasted a few years of this precious life in a direction that really wasn't mine.

Two options remained: the merchant marine or self-employment of some sort. Both seemed wonderfully liberating, but they appeared to be distant dreams, involving lengthy application processes. So, my father came up with the brave suggestion of taking over grandpa's roofing business. I believe my father's ideas were born as he spoke, and I still function the same way today. Dreaming up projects always opens the first door. And so, the next evening, I sat at grandpa and grandma's table pitching our vision to them, ecstatic that my new chapter was about to begin. My father made me feel like anything was possible and grandpa was ready for help. I felt the chains of captivity slipping from my ankles. I was in motion, taking responsibility for my big mouth. I was scared, scared as shit, but the feeling of freedom to make decisions, with all their consequences, was the freedom I was seeking.

But then...precisely then...came my call for conscription into the National Army. Damn it. Everyone expected it at some point, but it hit me like a ton of bricks. They were coming to take away a year and a half of my life, and the full force of their superiority was palpable down to the last bone. Here they were, the time thieves. And the feeling of having no choice is something I can only bear with great pain to this day.

Participating in this forced mental diarrhea called „conscription" and what I had to experience as a result of it during the fall of the Berlin Wall, became one of the reasons for my immigration to Canada later. Here, you can choose whether or not you want to be involved in the human conflict over religions or the disputes of old men to own the world. I always childishly thought that in the event of a war, I would be the one with the hotdog stand on the edge of the battlefield, but what choice I actually had would be communicated to me immediately. In Germany, at that time, „refusal" would have gotten me into a gulag-like situation and would have cost my father his job in the „National Olympic Team". I had already annoyed my father enough in sports.

The district command was in Annaberg, in an old villa that smelled of dictatorship and was simply cold. I was somewhat surprised when the people who were interviewing me seemed rather okay. Due to my automotive training, I was assessed as a driver for an officer in an artillery battalion somewhere in the middle of nowhere. At least that sounded somewhat less painful, and I was a bit relieved. What I didn't know back then was that those „pleasant" interviews all belonged to a larger strategy, one that I would painfully succumb to with my inexperienced young mind. More and more appointments came and conversations became interrogations. Looking back today, I for sure felt uncomfortable, but I still didn't suspect anything, who these soldiers with a lot of decoration on their shoulders really were. I was too young, blind and naive to see that this was actually not the army. I am still ashamed not to have recognized them... the 'Stasi'. The dangerous secret service had me by the neck.

UNDERCOVER

There I sat for the third appointment at a long table. Across, about 16 feet away from me was a bear in a uniform. Leaning forward slightly, he explained to me that the state needed me at the Berlin Wall, and asked me whether I would help prevent that those disloyal to „the system" stood a chance to flee the country. I stuttered some response that meant nothing, hoping it would keep me out of trouble.

I knew nothing about the Wall, but I could feel his questioning becoming more intense. He spoke to me until I was dizzy and cornered me precisely in the spot from which there were only two ways out in the GDR: big trouble or agreeing. He had me, he was good at his job. I made one more attempt, still believing he was from the army, and said that I didn't want to go to the Wall and I wouldn't shoot. Ice-cold stillness came over his face, and he closed his notes and left the room. Fuck... Now I was really scared. He left me waiting, waiting forever, and I could hear them talking through the walls, though of course not understanding anything. I was almost going crazy, and this feeling of being defenseless was preparing my capitulation. He came in with the words, „We reserve the right to call you up for military service whenever we deem necessary."

That meant they could interrupt my life at any time over the next 10 years and block basically everything you wanted to do or become. I meekly asked, „What do I have to do up there in Berlin?"

The appearance of my white flag of surrender made him friendlier again. He sat down, symbolically embraced me, and explained that everything was perfectly normal there. „The Wall is just regular military service, and everyone who goes there is already committed to preventing desertion by watching over each other. And if there's any suspicion, it's better to report it to a superior than to get in trouble." There was a short silence when he looked at me: „These can also be just family problems", he added.

It made sense to me to further prevent this escalation with this man. He handed me a paper on which I should choose a code name and sign. „Sign this, and you will be drafted next month. And if no one wants to run away, you won't hear from us again." I signed and left the torture chamber, dazed and with a firm handshake from a dark force.

About two hours later, in my father's garden, everything collapsed within me. I had described the whole thing to him, and when I finished, he said, „Are you crazy? You signed up for the Stasi!" At that time, I had no resistance left in me, and I burst into tears. For a long time, I held my head in my hands, too ashamed to look up. Eventually, he put his arm around me and began to tell me the story of his entry into „The Party".

Before the Olympic Games, for which he was nominated as a physiotherapist, they gave him a choice, basically on the gangway into the airplane,… Join the SED or stay at home. He chose „the book" because he loved sports and his job so much. We were both no traitors, but they had forced us into something from which individualists find it difficult to recover. You feel ashamed to have capitulated under pressure. You can certainly say that there were ways to defy them, but I was not brave enough for that. My life was too precious to me, and I was afraid of their radical methods.

It would have been best if they had never asked you, but once the Stasi had you on their radar, it was almost impossible to escape their network. Many years later, I would learn that the same had happened to many former athletes and friends. Of course, we all knew nothing about each other and it took years after the fall of the Berlin Wall for some light to be shed on this whole mess.

DRAFTED

It seemed like I had to postpone my plans to become my own boss by about a year and a half. At least that's what I thought, and they did too. And, once again, everything was going to turn out differently. Now, I want to tell you about one of the wildest times in my life, which could have gone very, very wrong.

So, I was standing at the train station ready for transport, and both my parents were with me on the platform. The face of a worried mother is something everyone knows. But the desperate 'you can't mess things up over there'-look from my father was unsettling. „You really need to keep quiet there now!" were the words of my loved ones, who I believe were very worried about me. The chance of me staying quiet there was practically non-existent, and they knew that, so they just hoped I would somehow get through it. And believe it or not, I really did try to stay silent and deaf to the army nonsense. Head down, bite my tongue, and soldier on.

I was sent to the Falkensee training regiment to prepare for the Wall, and that was the first time I couldn't keep quiet. Every morning they woke you up by ripping the door open and screaming as loud as possible. The room was freezing cold, and your neighbor farted while you put on your nice little outfit. Leather boots, gym shorts, and a shirt.

Then, we'd rush out, line up in formation and freeze. Now came the executioner. A young, low rank officer named „G", fresh from a special bootcamp and as dangerous as a jealous lover. He was someone who, at first sight, really wouldn't be my friend. He felt we were too loud, and we had to return to the barracks and back to bed. He repeated this two more times, despite the silence in the ranks. When hundreds of soldiers were back in formation, he stepped up on a podium and shouted, as we know it from German history, „Is there a problem?" He actually wanted to say, „My father never took me seriously." Then, my bottled up anger violently opened my mouth and out came: „Yes, you're still breathing." I have no idea where this came from. It was neither my style nor the right place. It was pure rage. „Who said that?" the ruler yelled. Cold fear rose within me, and I thought: „This is it, my end." But everybody remained silent, and so did I. We all just stood there, like frozen. What I didn't know until then was that some soldiers were supposed to leave on vacation after breakfast.

They left us all standing there hoping we would break, talked nonsense to us and threatened us with the worst case scenarios. And I stayed silent. After hours, the first wives gathered at the gate to pick up their loved ones to be a couple again for a two-day vacation. My fellow soldier beside me started to pressure me to admit it. The officers said „Nobody is going anywhere until this is found out". It seemed as if all my cards had been played, and my comrade-in-arms nudged me, whispering, „If you don't say it, I will say it now". I raised my head like a broken prisoner and whispered back, „Then say it, because I won't".

He didn't talk, and I still thank him and the entire battalion for that day. Thanks to you, I just narrowly escaped what could have been the biggest trouble of my life. After that, it was much easier for me to keep my mouth shut. At least for a little while.

BOOTCAMP

I'd like to dive a little deeper into this part of my life, as everything that defined the GDR, both materially and ideologically, no longer exists. I can't figure out why life put me on the global hotspot of those times, but it seems to be my story. From today's perspective, it's incredible how we dealt with the tension of an impending world war. During my time in the army, which began in August 1989, I had to not only pull my neck out of the hangman rope, but sometimes also had to burn the gallows down to get away. I won't write much about the basic training, where we experienced the brutality of this insane power structure. With very few exceptions, we had to deal with individuals who were utterly frustrated and desperate about their lives. Most officers were power tripping, unloading the rage on us lower ranks and nothing could ever happen to them.

The army, undoubtedly, was the largest gathering of emotionally starved people I've ever encountered, apart from today's industrial societies. But back then, at 20 years old, I just thought they were simply stupid or mean.

And after barely surviving the first action, I embarked on what would become the most significant and dangerous chapter of my life.

Shortly after I „joined" the East German Army, the first news blackout was imposed, and we were cut off from the world. No newspapers, no vacations, no radio. The country reeked of something enormously foul. And I, a free-thinking dreamer, had to keep myself in check because they were dangerous, „the militants". We had daily political brainwash sessions, discussions about socialism and our superior country. Four hours every day, and it seemed like all soldiers and officers had swallowed the „Ignorex pill" so that the unreasonable conversations would go smoothly. Some of the cooler soldiers had to actively shut off their brains to mumble a socialist answer – and they did. I just couldn't do it. Not because I wanted to be patriotic but it was too bizarre to be that theatrical. So, I got kicked out of these sessions 21 times, got yelled at, and rarely missed an opportunity to make the leader of the persuasion process lose his temper. And there it happened again. Someone good stepped into my life, a friend in a hopeless situation. My friend for this time... Sergeant „M".

I had to report to him every time I got suspended and he was chosen to figure out my punishment. Every single time. He could have done anything to me. I was so hated by the political officers that they would have considered any punishment justified. I was taken to his room, and he instructed me to clean it and then disappeared. I was always scared that something would finally break me, but nothing happened. Instead, Sergeant M would come and ask if I wanted tea. I could take off my cap and have tea with a real human. Sergeant M cared about me, and even though neither of us were gay, we immediately entered each other's comfort zones, where „hetero men" would usually feel a little uncomfortable. From that moment on, he watched over me and saved me from most of the torture. Some non-commissioned officers, I believe, waited until he was out of the house to get me. Mostly they made me jump up the stairs with a bag over my head and taunt me when I stumbled and fell down. But they had a whole bouquet of fun games in stock. One of those games was to squeeze me in a metal wardrobe, lock it and throw in a quarter. It was called „music box", because then I had to sing. I was claustrophobic and they didn't care.

TAKING A BREAK FOR INVESTIGATION

At this point in writing „I once was'" I had reason to interrupt the process, to further investigate a certain matter. During the post-reunification era there was a question that became an absolute moral dilemma in the East. Had your friend been involved with the Stasi, and did you want to know? There was no clear answer to this and many lifelong friendships were buried in those days. Some rightfully, because people caused harm by reporting about others, but many fell victim to an infiltrating unfair system that gave you very little chance not to be sucked into. I had made my own experiences with the authorities of our secret service, knowing that in most cases, it was almost impossible or came with brutal consequences not to be associated with the Stasi if they had chosen to ask you. But in my case, I wanted to know how genuine my relationship with Sergeant M truly was. It was crucial for me and important for the book.

It took a couple of years for me to return to writing. During that time, I had found Sergeant M and my answer in Berlin, crossed Canada in a school bus powered by vegetable oil, and lived through numerous health and spiritual highs and lows - probably enough material for two or three more books. Now, I'm back on my sofa in Yukon, and it's time to continue. Grab a glass of red wine, make yourself comfortable and let's keep going.

Autumn 1989, the training regiment in Falkensee. Doubts about Sergeant M began on a day that was quite likely the hottest in the period leading up to the fall of the Berlin Wall. My point of view was that of the lowest ranking soldier in an army who was challenging not just its own nation, but took on the whole world.

We were with about 15 soldiers in our room. No one really knew what was happening at the front, and we were all too young and inexperienced to even remotely grasp the true extent. A major suddenly appeared in our room, he was someone I couldn't stand to the core. He had knocked out a tooth of a friend during a self-defense demonstration. I had to choke down all my anger back then to refrain from attacking him. So this disturbed individual, now a decision-maker on war and peace, entered our room, was saluted, and began to speak. „The demonstrators will try to march from Alexanderplatz Berlin with mothers and children in the lead, towards Brandenburg Gate and provoke a breakthrough." In other words, you, in your trench, receive the message: they're coming now. The world doesn't spin in these moments, only your stomach turns. But our major wasn't done. „You will receive double the ammunition (four clips instead of two) and position yourselves in front of the gate. What will you do if they come towards you?" Silence. All eyes rolled to the floor and got lost in reading the mouse-gray linoleum. More silence.

And then me. „I will not shoot, and if all else fails, I will run through the gate." Then the silence deepened into a coma. Refusal to obey orders. Crap. „Soldier Haustein, would you like to reconsider your answer?" „Y-yes... I would take my machine gun with me to ensure nobody gets hurt?" More crap. But it had been said.

They arrested and escorted me to the Stasi cellar. Everything from there on was like a movie. I, the prisoner, standing with my captor in front of a coded door with no handle. And then it happened. The door opened, and Sergeant M emerged, but only half-way. Then a hand from behind grabbed him and pulled him back in, and the door slammed shut like a guillotine. Bang. The situation plummeted from aw-ful to „fuuuck" in free fall. Him? What was he doing here? Was he not on my side anymore? The door opened again, and another official ordered me to come in. Sergeant M was nowhere to be seen. I was led into a room, and there I waited. An older, obvi-ously high ranking officer came in and asked me not to get up to salut. He was half in uniform and half in an undershirt, offered me a cigarette and asked me if I wanted a coffee. The emotional mary-go-round of the last 10 minutes tore from its foundation. From escape, fear, anger, surprise, regret to „oh yes, give me drugs". Cigarettes and coffee help any non-smoker on the gallows.

The interrogation was anything but what you'd ex-pect. It was just him and me. He knew a lot about me, knew all my friends in my hometown of Ober-wiesenthal. He also knew about my endless escapades with the political educators. But above all, he knew one thing. Our country was starting to move, stretching itself towards freedom, and he knew that the old kings weren't truly at the helm anymore. He could have done anything he wanted with me in there, anything. This was the situation where young soldiers disappeared into torture camps, or where they made you simply disappear. But he didn't do any of this; no shouting, no threats. He remained friendly and understanding. I didn't care whether it was a strategy or not. I took the moment as it was.

We were very open with each other, almost affectionate. It was a situation that probably occurs at the end of many wars. The theater disappears, and the truth emerges. The coffee and cigarette contributed to a bizarre kind of hazy relaxation. It felt like a snake getting stoned with a mouse.

He advised me not to stir up any more dust and to avoid any kind of confrontation with certain superiors. He knew these people longer than I did and he understood their danger. He could only hint at it, it was more a gesture but he, quite elegantly so, made sure that I got the memo. As our conversation drew to a close, I felt connected to him. There were humans in this army who were true socialists. There were the heroic people of our nation who kept the peace in the streets. But there were also good men on the „inside" like him, who helped to make this a „peaceful revolution".

I'd like to mention that all of this didn't happen at the Wall yet. At this moment in time, we're still in the three-month basic training at the bootcamp regiment. The „monday demonstrations" in the streets are in full swing, but the Wall stands untouched, the shoot-to-kill order is a reality, and my transfer to the front-line of the Wall itself is imminent.

The day wasn't over yet. I can't remember our fare-well exactly, but there was a closeness between us. A vital closeness. He handed me over to a subordinate officer in the next room with the order to take me back to my company. This officer immediately screamed at me that I should salute my superior. Re-luctantly, he and I both assumed the designated pos-ture for this static interaction and got it over with. „Major, may I be dismissed?" „Dismissed, soldier..."

As I was led out of the cellar and reached the bar-racks yard, I saw all the soldiers were on the trucks. Many soldiers, many Kalashnikov machine guns, many trucks. We passed my buddies, and I saw Ser-geant M on one of the trucks. Then we walked past the major whom I had refused the order in the first place. We just walked by and I kept my head down. My escort ordered me to go on guard duty in the fa-cility. The trucks drove away. Everyone drove away to guard the Wall while I was left home on duty, without a weapon, alone in front of empty barracks.

Sergeant „M" was not in the secret service. He was a very good man who believed in the kindness of so-cialism and in our nation. Over time, he went from Sergeant „M" to just „M", we remained friends and when we talk about those times we get ice cold shiv-ers and can't believe how close it was to become a tragedy no-one would have recovered from, and to think we were just kids back then.

THE WALL

After my special bootcamp time in Falkensee, I was transferred to the border regiment, which meant: duty at the Berlin Wall. When we entered the new barracks for the first time, they showed us the memorial room of a soldier who had fallen here during his duty. His bed, his uniform, his belongings – a warning shot to the heart for us and our upcoming tasks. The notion of what had happened at the Wall left little room to breathe, and all that remained was the hope that I could somehow avoid being where the trouble was. But there had already been 53 people shot at that border; who knows what was really going down there.

The NVA (National People's Army) was a madhouse where ranks meant absolute power. Someone with triggering eyes, like me, sparked an urgent desire in every frustrated superior to put me into place. This vulnerability led to many nights under my blanket, quietly crying, and often the thought arising of not being able to endure it. But there was no alternative in a still-functioning army. I had to surrender, and they enjoyed watching me reluctantly swallow their poison. Additionally, one was immediately tormented by the „three-year-olds", a special kind of soldiers who had signed up for a longer draft and had privileges coming with this. Them, and the ones who were going home soon and had done their time, enjoyed the unsupervised right to torture us. We were unprotected and at their mercy. From being locked in and having to sing for them to really terrible and inhuman things, people like me had to experience the full program of dictatorial misery and personal rage.

And so it began – my duty in the high-security area in the heart of Europe. When I stood for the first time in front of the „imperialist barrier", what the Wall was called from our side, carrying my Kalashnikov and the order to shoot, I noticed instantly that the defense systems were pointing in the wrong direction. All fences, climb barriers, alarm systems, and electric fences were facing us, towards my country. Meanwhile, our „enemy" was able to walk up to the Wall with a hardware store ladder, while a raked sand strip kept us away from it. I was so confused. I thought our job was to keep the Westerners away, but the truth was that we kept our own people from escaping.

Standing in this no man's land, with the task of keeping it untouched, gave birth to the feeling of not being in real life. A state that transforms people into soldiers in every war. For the first time, I realized that these emergency situations do not happen in a humanly comprehensible reality but in a blurred state of fear. In this insane level of tension, everything was possible. The fear of having to take responsibility and live with the horrific consequences later in real life made all my senses awaken to the utmost. I decided that nothing would happen... nothing... at any cost.

My border Trabi called "The Bucket"

MY OWN WALL

I served in Potsdam in the Border Regiment. As
mentioned before, border duties were a bizarre thing.
They started by dividing 24 hours by 3, is 8. That
made eight hours of 'Wall time' and about one hour
for preparation and debriefing. Depending on winter
or summer orders, you dressed appropriately, smug-
gling as many forbidden things into your clothes as
possible – things like candles, small books, and su-
per-forbidden radios. You never knew in advance
where the border shift would take place, which was
part of the control tactic of our „system". It began
with the weapon handover, two clips full of bullets,
and a Russian indestructible assault and swamp rifle.
To be honest, carrying a weapon was not unpleasant.
The consequences of using such a weapon had been
pushed far into unreality, and the inexplicable feeling
that having a rifle was better than not having one
prevailed. It feels a bit strange in hindsight, but that's
how it was; sorry.

Then followed preparation for the gathering of the
soldiers. I was a driver, so now I had to get my com-
bat Trabant from the garage. I still have a picture of
it. The coolest convertible the socialists ever built.
These Trabants were equipped with a wonderful
heater, which didn't work in our regiment because
the higher-ranking officers had removed an essential
part to use in their own cars. Spare parts were like
gold in our country.

Without the heater, this tent on wheels became a super refrigerator during the winter. But it wasn't

always cold. So, I brought the Trabi out and headed to the gathering place. There, all foot soldiers, motorcycles, trucks, and Trabis lined up in a horseshoe shape to receive the daily orders and to swear the oath to obey those. A shouting officer stood in the middle, and we pledged that we would allow no one to enter or leave the country, even at the risk of our own lives. No one really listened because, in case of trouble, we were screwed anyway, with or without the oath. The most exciting part of the event for me was the dogs of the dog squad. The dogs were super excited to jump on the trucks. They loved duty above all else but were too submissive and well-trained to move. So, they sat in a sitting position, sometimes almost a hundred of them. Not making a sound but bursting with excitement.

At this point, I hopelessly fell in love with dogs. Now, as I write these words to you, I have nine Huskies sitting in the garden, waiting for me to finally put down the book and harness them up so we can explode out of the yard into the wilderness. All my love for dogs began there, on that assembly square in Berlin, where the loyal souls of the Wall dogs dug themselves into my heart.

Once, I disrupted an assembly. It was Christmas time, and I was a bit late for the vehicle lineup. So late that they had to wait for me. But I wasn't done decorating my Trabant yet. I had Christmas ornaments on the antenna, tinsel and decoration everywhere and a candle on the dashboard. I could only drive slowly to the square, or the candle would go out. As I rolled into position, I turned off the engine and stood next to the vehicle. It got very quiet when all eyes fell on my 'sleigh'. I stared straight ahead and didn't make a move. It was just wonderful – hundreds of soldiers began to smile. Fortunately, I had hit the Christmas nerve just right. Despite the seriousness of the socialist border protection measures, the majority couldn't help but think of their loved ones at home. Incense, good food, traditions and of course, the wives' undergarments, that were hopefully not being messed with by a neighbor. What were we doing here anyway? Well, that question didn't arise in a dictatorship. But the sudden Christmas ambush brought a glow to everyone's eyes. Naturally, I was politely shouted at and had to change the decoration, but there was no punishment.

Then it started. Everyone on the vehicles, speeding through Berlin until they found the section of the Wall they had to protect. Again, line up, loading weapons, and then we entered the death zone. The previous shift now reported that nothing had happened, and everyone found their section and began their duty. Well, there is much to tell about this time. I witnessed the complete collapse of the GDR and the Wall, from normal border duty in the intact republic with shoot-to-kill orders, to the transformation of the no-man's-land into the International Hiking Trail. I can't tell you everything, but I will guide you through what have been the most moving stories for me. Fortunately, and I want to say this right at the beginning, I never had to shoot. But I can also say that we didn't shoot, bending orders and adjusting to very fast changes. Here are two stories that

can probably be called „inside stories" from the fall
of the Berlin Wall. In both, looking back on it today,
I was a hero and an idiot at the same time. This mix-
ture probably prevented the worst. Today, I always
see parallels to Forrest Gump. You don't know how
you got into the situation, but once you're here, the
logical steps unfold.

So, story one: border duty in a section of the Wall
with a 90-degree corner. These corners were the first
places where Wall-peckers from the west side
chipped away souvenirs and made small holes in the
process. I was on the patrol road, waiting for my
leading officer, who had climbed up an observation
tower to warm up with his buddies up there. I looked
at the small hole in the Wall when a little boy from
the west side crawled through it and suddenly stood
on the death strip (also called the no-go land). This
section was about 30 meters wide, machine-raked
sand, footprint-free, possibly mined, and undoubtedly an absolute „no-go" for everyone. There he
stood. Alone, with his LA Raider Baseball Cap and
his giant eyes. Through the hole, an arm was fumbling, obviously making a great effort to pull the little
one back through the Wall, but Junior had gone
about 6 feet too far. I leaned my machine gun against
my car and started walking towards the little boy. The
first thing that came to my mind was the land mines.
Some said there were never any, and others claimed
the opposite. Sometimes we saw a strange-looking
tractor driving over the sand to smooth it perfectly.
The tractors never exploded, but that wasn't very reassuring. My heart almost flew out of my chest, but I

kept going. Suddenly, I felt that I was now the one making tracks on the forbidden sand while also walking towards the Wall. These were the situations in which soldiers in the past had shot soldiers. Certainly, the political situation had somewhat softened our shoot-to-kill order, but it still existed, and I was just finding out if it still applied. I kept going. Then the windows of the observation towers flew open, and weapons were audibly loaded. I didn't turn around, and the command „Border guard! Stop or I will shoot!" didn't come. I was now in front of the little one. He was frozen stiff with fear. Although he was a little child, he understood perfectly that the world he had just entered into through the small hole was life-threatening. The silence and the tension radiating from the towers were paralyzing. I grabbed the child and stuffed him back into his world, through the Wall. His father took him from my hands and probably had the happiest moment of his life. He was not unaware, he explained to me in half English, half German. He was a former Marine of the American occupation zone and had served on the other side. When he heard about the possible fall of the Wall back home in the USA, he flew over to witness it, and in the process, his little one had escaped.

As a heartfelt thanks, he handed me his son's cap through the Wall, and I gave him my 'bear's vagina'. That was the unofficial name for the border troops' winter hat. As I walked away, trying to find my own footprints to get around a possible minefield, I saw for the first time in what a terrible situation the other soldiers had been. All of them aiming for us, all of them making decisions about life and death. When I returned to the patrol road, everyone started breathing again. Those from the tower, including my officer, tumbled down the iron ladder, and I got my verbal reprimand. They now had the job of reporting this international incident to their superiors and explaining their behavior. And I, the little foot soldier, sunk into my car seat and tried to grasp what had just happened. But that took a while. What I could celebrate right away was my new baseball cap. At least the LA Raiders would have been proud of me. I wore that thing for many years until it eventually dissolved on my head. I often think of the little boy today. Maybe he's playing baseball; he should be around 40 now.

Visitors to the border line

President „Honnie" as the Santa Claus

Die Grenzgebietsschilder haben sie
abgebaut und gleich unter sich verteilt.
Die Bevölkerung hat den Soldaten Schnapss
ausgeschänkt bei jedem Schild.
Heute habe ich Euer Packet erhalten
Vielen Dank für die vielen schönen
Sachen. Auch noch mal vielen Dank
für das was Nadine mir mit gegeben
hat. Der Baumschmuck und das Männl
ist verkauft. Die Kerze die mich wärmt
ist jetzt fast abgebrannt und mein Dienst
neigt dem Ende. Nächster Urlaub ist
voraussichtlich 15-21 Dez. Da ist übrigens
auch Nürnberger Christkindelmarkt. Bob
hat mir geschrieben. Ihm geht es genau
so gut wie es mir ging. So warten wir
ab was passiert und halten mir die Daumen

Tschüss Euer Holger
439 Tage

Liebe Eltern, liebe Melli[?]

Ich schreibe Euch gleich von meinem 1.
Grenzdienst wieder. Ich habe Nachtdienst
und ich sitze auf in einem Turm am See
Es ist ziemlich kalt aber das macht nichts
denn es hat sich viel verändert. Die Stimmung
ist eine ganz andere wie vor dem Urlaub.
Ein paar Anlagen und schon verschwinden
und auch so geht es viel viel lockerer zu
als sonst. Fast stündlich kommen neue Befehle
raus die den Grenzdienst erleichtern.

Ein paar Leute haben sie schon abgezogen
und es soll weiter gehen. drastisch Von
150 auf 50 pro Einheit und wir werden
wieder Zoll zum 12 Parteitag. Die Politr
sind völlig von der Rolle und hören uns
jetzt zu. Zivil wo's geht und fahren in den
Westteil kann auch noch kommen. In
Potsdam fahren Westberliner Doppelstock-
busse Linienverkehr. Man kann ein-
steigen und ab. McDonald's holt seine
Gäste auch hier ab.

Letter to my parents

History

My wall

THE FORBIDDEN TRIP

My second story took place in one of the most special sections that the border line had to offer. It was either in Kleinmachnow or Klein Glienicke, more likely the latter. You can surely envision the village of the Gauls from Asterix and Obelix. Such locations existed at the Wall too. They were bubble-shaped, almost completely closed protrusions into the other Germany, with a very small entrance from our side. These enclaves were like small countries within our own. They were as big as a mini-village, surrounded by a double wall with many intermediate gates and equipped with an additional security code system. Entry into these areas was like crossing a border, requiring identification and such.

In these small separate worlds, due to their strategic uniqueness, only loyalists to the regime with their families resided. Inside, it was like a fairytale land. They had small schools, the finest old villas, small shops, a pub, and sometimes even a small cemetery. Not many were allowed in, not even us. Of course, I cheekily went to take a look. Thinking about it now, I realize it's quite a delight that I can tell you all of this today. Everything was super top-secret, and I was „James Blond". I don't know what they were thinking, placing me there.

These special border areas were simultaneously terrifying and romantic. Like a fairytale forest surrounded by a high-security prison wall. Parallel walls, 14 feet high and about 60 feet apart, with a border path in between, steel gates every few hundred meters, separating one section from another. You could only see the sky when you were inside.

So, I was in one of these boxes with another private. In the dark of the night, with nothing to look at, we discovered a hole in the Wall to The West. In and of itself, nothing we hadn't seen before, but this time everything was different. We looked at each other, and slowly the ghostly truth dawned on us that we were all alone with that hole. Behind us and in front of us, the Wall, and on both sides, the high-security gates that could only be opened by us, with a code only we had, and only after prior notice. And suddenly, we, two little soldiers, had complete control over a piece of the Berlin Wall with an opening to The West. Our blood stopped as we looked into each other's eyes and back at the hole. Well, guess what happened next. After a brief silent agreement of trust, we went through the hole.

When we, the two Wall soldiers, on the other side, straightened our uniforms and adjusted our rifles, we were in The West. The 'everything is different - West'. The West, where products smelled good, where cars were for sale, and colorful pictures were in the newspapers. The West, that wanted to kill us, and where drug addicts lay dead in the washrooms of the train station. The world where their German Mark could buy ten times as much as ours, and where Phil Collins played so loudly that it could be heard even in our Berlin. And we came from a hole, behind which they would have shot us for what we had just done.

The hole suddenly looked very different. As we woke up from our standstill coma, we began to look around like two frontline scouts. We had landed in a kind of housing development. The houses all looked new, with paint on them and fine roofs. Remember, I was a roofer! No one was in sight, and we began to penetrate deeper into this unknown land. A dog barking and coming at us scared us out of our minds but was stopped by a fence. We walked on and came to a house without a fence and another dog, and probably it was me who had the brilliant idea: "Come on, let's ring the bell".

So, I said it and I rang it. The door opened, and a John Lennon type with round glasses said, „Yes, please?". Then his eyes got bigger than his round glasses and fear took over the moment. I quickly realized that we did not look very lovely with our uniforms and our AK-47's. I assured him that we came in peace and he would do us a huge favor if he didn't freak out and could just let us in now. Silently, he stepped aside, and we entered the house. His wife and daughter immediately knew that something big had happened and came to look at us. The man ordered his daughter to go to her room and to not come out. His wife and he took seats on two chairs. They felt threatened and highly uncomfortable. We put down the rifles and tried to cool the situation, starting to tell how this historic meeting came about. Slowly, we all became aware that world history was happening right then and there. The kind of history that would be written about in books later, and people would say, „I was there!". Then we had tea.

We talked about the Wall and how everything looked from their side, and about that they were teachers. Probably every other sentence was an incredulity statement that this was really happening. Then, politely, he asked if he could take a photo. We felt honored and posed with them, like old friends who had just come home from the war. The excitement and the constant glances at our walkie-talkies soon made us restless, and we thanked them and said our goodbyes. Not long after, another slip through the hole ended our first visit to The West, and it was probably the only time in the history of the Wall that entering the high-security area created a feeling of being safe again. Madness, we had visited The West, and no one had noticed. And we came back, and no one had noticed – crazy!

The rest of the shift was an adrenaline cocktail of orgasmic proportions - mixed with doubt, pride, incomprehension and ended with folded hands and the wish to the universe that the teacher wouldn't send the pictures to the newspaper the next morning. He didn't, the good man. He sent them to me about a year after the fall of the Wall when everything was safe. Thank you very much, my friend. I visited the family two more times in a unified Germany. We always drank tea and rejoiced in our shared history. Their surroundings changed dramatically with the fall of the Wall. The beautiful east villas now were occupied by nouveau riche people, and nothing reminds us of the gray wall behind the teacher's house, where their good-smelling tea was served.

CHANGING THE FLAG

The East German army consisted of quite an interesting bunch in those days. So, after the events and stories that I just told you, the following happened. Suddenly, as members of the East German army, we were allowed to go to the west part of Berlin during our off-duty hours. Just to make that clear, we went to another country for a drink, dressed in our military uniforms and with our military ID's, while in border service we were defending our Wall and country with shoot-to-kill orders. Total madness, right? Here's another example of what was possible behind the Iron Curtain at that time. I had acquired an East German border sign. You know, the ones that said, „Stop! State border! Do not proceed, you are leaving the Soviet sector!" A popular souvenir during that time. Anyway, I got one and took it with me on a trip to West Berlin. There are plenty of junk shops there that buy and sell everything. So, I went in with my sign and came out with a Confederate flag. I had always liked that flag and the music coming from that country. I even got some West German marks on top of it. Unfortunately, I have to admit that as a 19-year-old East German, I had no clue about the Civil War between the North and the South. The dealer probably collapsed in laughter with his sign, just like our Wall eventually did.

Now, my friend and I turned the Western money into beer and Schnapps, and then we took the double-decker bus back to the barracks. The beer had its effect, and we needed it. No one can endure so much change without alcohol. We were right in the middle of the playground of history. No one knew what was really going on. So, we staggered past the Military Police with our new banner under our arms and wobbled towards our quarters. As we passed the main parade ground, the flagpole caught my eye for a moment. Wait a minute. Or better: „Waaait a momeeent…" hiccup... Have you ever drunkenly looked up at a flagpole? It wobbles, and then it knocks you over. There it stood, the mast with the fluttering East German flag. Sacred and untouched like President Honecker's pictures.

It felt a bit strange when we lowered it slowly, the black, red, and gold with the emblem in the middle. Usually, it stopped at half-mast when someone important had died, and then it went back up, flying proudly for the idea of socialism. But this time, it came all the way down and was replaced by my new flag. And so, the soldiers marched the next morning, until it was noticed by the authorities, under a different flag. I had hidden the original flag in my room. So, after all that turmoil, I had traded an East German border sign for an East German flag. That's how crazy the time was when the Wall around our Berlin fell.

STEALING A DOG

Slowly, the army began to dissolve. The border troops were supposed to become customs officers again. This meant that we were to complete our mandatory military service in full. In that autumn, a massive storm hit, and I have to mention that I, Holly, was a roofer just like our now-ex-president. The wind had destroyed hundreds of roofs in Germany, so I wrote a request for discharge. With the reasoning that my grandfather needed me in the family business, I tried to get out of this madhouse before someone would be completely losing it. During this time, the relief that everything was somewhat more relaxed was significantly overshadowed by the growing fear among the officers. At the end of a war, even if it was just a cold one, everything they had done to others before could now come back to haunt them. The tension was rising. My discharge request went unanswered. And worse, on my last day, which I didn't know was the last, I was transferred to the Pioneers, a unit tasked with dismantling the border installations and therefore had zero chance of any early release. Since I was the only one transferred, I believe that this relocation was a personal act of revenge by an officer who didn't like me.

So, I moved to a new regiment with my belongings and still had border duty on that particular day. My last shift on the Wall that changed so many lives ended in an early morning snowstorm, and I went back to my old regiment to return my weapon. The weapon was taken from me, and I, completely exhausted, was sent back to the barracks courtyard to shovel snow alone at 5 a.m. Something was off, but I couldn't put my finger on it. But they, for sure, were talking about me inside. When I had hidden most of the snow, I went in and was immediately called even further inside, into the room of the officer on duty.

To my surprise, I received my final order: „By eleven hundred, you are to leave the premises. Your service time is over. Turn in your belongings. Dismissed!" He almost had to push me away; that's how rigid I stood. I immediately knew that I didn't want to ask any questions and just do what the man had said. And maybe I would have been able to do everything before eleven hundred... If it weren't for Bessy.

Bessy was a pitch-black German Shepherd, one of the best-trained guard dogs. She belonged to a soldier nicknamed „Skinny", whose mandatory service ended before mine. When saying goodbye to my friend Skinny, he asked me to take care of Bessy. Many guard dogs were euthanized during that time. The good ones, of course, weren't, but he was worried about his dear Bessy. And so, bypassing the chain of command, I had claimed Bessy for myself and had been taking her on border duty for some time. Like a proper dog handler. No one noticed, and my border duty became much more enjoyable with her. She liked to drink, carried my stuff in two pouches I had converted into dog saddlebags, and to this day, she remains the only dog I know who liked wearing a hat. She made me feel so safe and was the kindest weapon I ever met, and we were in love.

So my highly welcomed dismissal from this mess coincided with bidding farewell to Bessy. No soldier had ever been able to take a dog home. The dogs were very valuable and bearers of secrets. The situation was hopeless, simply because I had a few hours of running around ahead of me to return everything the army had loaned me. So, I decided to steal her or do something later. I had to get out first.

That's when I remembered the encounter with a federal policeman from West Berlin at the Wall. We had met through the two dogs we were handling. He had heard that the West police would like to buy our dogs if our dog unit was disbanded. In my desperate situation, I decided to start with this disbandment immediately. But how? It made no sense to ask anyone in my regiment. Soldier Holly was not popular enough to let him steal a dog. Besides, officially, I didn't even have a dog. And so, with my last clean collar tab, absolutely correct uniform, and with incredible courage and stoic naivety, I marched to the commander of our border section. I knew he was a general but confirmed it once again with his beautiful receptionist soldieress. „I would like to speak to General regarding the dog unit". A „Yes, sir" followed. To my surprise, I was let in. I played my part, and the big man remained half-out of his uniform and, in my opinion, drunk behind the antique desk. I told him about my dismissal and that I knew we were allowed to buy our dogs because the dog unit was being disbanded. Ohhh, thin ice, very thin ice, such a carpet of lies. I also told him that they didn't want to give me the dog because they didn't like me. Oh, even thinner ice. Hopefully, he says something soon. The old general didn't look good. The impending loss of his beloved shoulder boards was written all over his face. For a moment, I thought he would devour me and put my bones in the dog kennel. Then the old warrior stood up and cursed, „This is unheard of!" I could only think: „What now? Them or me?" But I kept my mouth shut. He went to the gray telephone and grunted, „Just wait". When the commander of the dog unit answered on the other end, my general shouted into the receiver, „Immediately hand over the dog to soldier Haustein!" Bang... the receiver flew down, making the gray telephone turn all red. If he had waited for the reply from the other end, everything would have been exposed. But that response got stuck in the secret pipeline until today. „Dismissed!" As a thank-you, I shook his hand - and I think he really noticed that I was grateful. He was for sure a bit stunned. Then, with a proper soldier-like greeting, I left the highest-ranking military who had ever trusted me. Well... as Lenin once said: Trust is good, but dogs are better.

And so, at exactly 11 am, I fled with my backpack and my dog, traditionally tossing some change backward over the exit gate. A parting ritual for no return. At the train station, I bought a small 0.3-liter bottle of vodka and went to the wrong train. On purpose. I thought they would come for me or at least follow. And with every policeman who appeared in my way, I changed direction. On the train, I poured the vodka over my paranoid soul and fell asleep. Bessy roamed freely in the train when I woke up at Leipzig's train station. I had the greatest difficulty orienting myself. But no one seemed to be looking for me. I went to Zwickau and took a taxi to Cainsdorf. Home.

Now I was the one coming home, just like my great-grandfather from the first and my grandfather and his brother from the second World War. For some reason, I had expected a warm welcome. I had forgotten that they didn't even know I was coming. I found the house empty, emptier than I could bear. I found myself unwelcomed and crying like a baby with my bewildered Wall dog on the basement stairs. So, that was it, the end of my country as I knew it. I sat on the same stairs again, which I had left seven months ago, and nothing was the same anymore. The world was unrecognizable. I hugged my dog.

Bessy and I in „No man's land"

The two of us finally at home

TRANSITIONING THE HARD WAY

In the book it is now 1990. That sounds like yesterday, feels like yesterday, and yet it's already been so
many years since. 5 years is nothing; in 10, a lot usually changes. But 20 or 30 is a substantial chunk of
time, and little Holly has by now, 2024, transformed
from an East German car mechanic/roofer at the
end of the Cold War into a Canadian song- and
book-writing wanderer of forests and worlds. And a
father of two is he as well.

So, summarizing the present briefly, I've experienced
half of my life in socialism and the other half in capitalism. I feel very fortunate that everything unfolded
as it did.

My GDR (German Democratic Republic), as I knew
it before the Cold War, was wonderful. There were
many comforts for young people. Additionally, there
was little traffic, cheap alcohol, and no strange drug
pitfalls. The lack of travel and political freedom had-
n't yet fully registered for me. Plus, we had time.
Waiting was one of the fundamental qualities of East
Germans, something we didn't even feel strained
about. We were more confused when things went
smoothly and quickly. And now, in the new Germany, everything moved fast. So fast that most people over 50 struggled not to lose their footing under
the new quality knockoff shoes. A significant part of
the core population began to leave the country.
Those who stayed are still mostly here today. I stayed
too. At least for a long time. Strangely, the West
never really captured my heart back then.

It smelled good there, but not as familiar as home. The people were probably okay, but since we had to learn their system, we were the fools. From a capitalist perspective, we were indeed clueless. We didn't know how things worked. And so, we sat there, and the West directed us to the desired corners. All the structures we had learned were dismantled. People who were important were no longer, and others took over the ship mostly with their own crew. Stores, cooperatives, and businesses closed so fast that by now you could buy food here and insurance there. We would have probably done the same to the West as they did to us. They were just the stronger system.

Here's a small example that illustrates that it wasn't about quality – it was about the system. My father was the physiotherapist for the Olympic GDR Luge team for 25 years. He also supported ski jumpers, cross-country skiers, and bobsledders at many Olympics and World Championships. He wasn't just the muscle relaxer but also the equipment carrier, peace judge, shoulder to cry on, and friend. Above all, he was an excellent therapist and always enjoyed his work. Oh, almost forgot: he was also very affordable. With the stack of medals these teams had earned, not even the Klondike Gold Rush could compete. With the Cold War's end, a little letter arrived in my dad's shivering hands... and it was over.

The Western therapist got the job, and my father received a - now capitalistic and much colder - handshake with the words, „We are sure you will manage". My father managed to make it again and retired many years later as an accomplished independent physiotherapist. Many world-class athletes still came to him for many years, even if they had to take some detours ski-flying for it.

LIVING WITH MY GRANDPARENTS

So, I lived in my grandparents' house again. I really liked it there. They had an old but very spacious house. The roofing business was attached to the house, and after that, in a kind of Matryoshka-style, increasingly smaller buildings followed until the entire property was filled. Our business was founded in 1936, so everyone knew us. Additionally, since its founding, everything that could be even remotely reused had been collected; everything else initially went into an extra shed. We had wooden ladder scaffolds, two Trabant station wagons, and two trailers, one of which was a decapitated truck so, it wasn't clear who was pulling whom here. Perhaps our most significant wealth was an assortment of old roof tiles that were no longer in production. Unexpectedly, these would benefit us greatly because there were many old roofs that needed repairs for many years after the Cold War. Consequently, all these contracts stayed with local firms because the Westerners simply didn't have the material for it. And so began my career in the fresh post-reunification chaos in little Cainsdorf.

I wanted to become a roofer, or rather, I wanted to be independent. I would have driven any boss crazy anyway, so I preferred to take responsibility for my own mess. My grandfather's business was perfect for that. He was glad that I wanted to continue, and I was glad that he showed me everything he had learned in the last 60 years.

Being a roofer was good in the GDR. Although there was hardly any material, when it rained inside people's homes, a kind of panic set in, in which the craftsman appeared as a celebrated savior, reassuring the lady of the house and temporarily sealing the hole in the roof with a piece of gum, risking his life.

I had worked with my grandpa as a little boy, and I always found it terribly exciting to be on the roofs of a city or to see what people had accumulated in their attics. Besides, there was always food where you worked, and people were grateful that you came to help them. At least that's how it was in the old times.

The Erxleben house and my grandfather's roofing business

BABY STEPS ON NEW GROUND

At the beginning, I didn't know much about roofing, so I attended every opportunity for further education that presented itself. And suddenly, there were so many options available. From trips to slate mines with subsequent wine tasting, trade fair visits with free sausages, to personal consultations in our own home. All of a sudden, the customer was king. And let me tell you, dear readers, that was very pleasant. Wherever we learned something or bought materials, we received little gifts and coffees to deepen the friendship with the product. Initially, they sold us so much crap cause we had to figure out what works and what not. But foremost we made the quantum leap from „Can I have this product if I get you two crates of special beer?" to "We would be extremely pleased to welcome you as a customer." It took a while to learn to take that seriously. And so, all the roofers happily started working. As quickly as we became kings as customers, our customers also transformed into queens. For example, on the day before the introduction of the German West Mark, people paid their bills at night on our doorstep in East cash, knowing that all banks were closed, and the money would devalue 90% overnight. That really hurt, as the work was done in full.

During this time, a very delightful human joined my inner circle: Uwe, the milkman. For years, he had driven milk to the stores before the cows even got up, and under the tarp of his W50 truck, there were often GDR black-market products. And these had to be distributed before anybody woke up. However, the black market and the profession of a milkman were abolished, and Uwe needed a new playing field. He decided to become a roof building material dealer, and that's how our paths crossed. He had not the slightest idea about it, and since I also had little knowledge of the trade, we complemented each other brilliantly. I became his customer, and I am to this day. I still have some tools from him laying around, because neither he nor I could ever figure out what to do with them. So, we both managed to get by, sharing what the other had found out, getting each other work, and looking as if we knew what we were doing. Well, we certainly made an effort. Uwe is still one of the best actors and skilled individuals I know. A gentleman through and through, with a very elegant language and the conviction of a winner. He couldn't play an instrument but conducted the entire symphony. Uwe was an honorable man and still is today and I learned a whole lot from him. All his employees have stayed with him. Who can say that about themselves?

What truly connected us, however, was our humor. Often, after finishing work, we went to a regulars' table in a pub and told people fairy tales about us until the rafters bent. Two Munchhausens were sometimes a bit much, but always very funny. For example, we (usually unrehearsed) presented ourselves as rabbit breeders, drag lift owners, or I introduced myself as the son from his first marriage. The resulting conversation was always new for all those involved. For example, it happened that people suddenly remembered an old drag lift, even though there was no mountain there. Or they remembered Uwe's first wife who never existed.

And so, the time of new beginnings, which was really exhausting and uncertain, was much easier to endure because of our friendship. He had my back and I had his. He also elevated my status among the ranks of master roofers because he acknowledged our friendship. He was one of the „old guard", and I was very young. The old masters didn't have the greatest respect for me because I was new.

OPA

For me, during that time, there was only one direction, and that direction was forward. I absorbed the job like a sponge, tried to do really good work, and always enjoyed how well my grandpa was received by people. He was truly a sociable companion. While his brother had built a roofing empire a few cities away, my grandpa focused on tranquility. A beer here, a talk there. Old Helmar could tell many stories, most from the war and the rest about football. Much later, shortly before his death, he only lived in these two worlds. Football and war mixed with a dose of Alzheimer's. Goebbels had stormed and Rummenigge had been captured. I'll tell you a nice story about Helmar's death later. Now, back to life.

Helm, as everyone called him, was a laid-back teacher. He was not a boss, so it was more like an outing to the neighbors than a work assignment. If it rained, no fumbling around was done, and everyone stayed home. And on Fridays, punctually at 1 pm, we disappeared to the lake for camping and beer drinking. He lived a modest life, but he had found where the golden middle ground was. The place where you find the greatest treasure of all: time. My grandpa always had time. Haste was foreign to him and made him feel uncomfortable. He remained true to himself his whole life and took his time. Perhaps that's why our connection was so fruitful and long-lasting. I could rush ahead, and he was glad that someone was rushing, but not him. Of course, we also had generational problems that stood between us in this time of upheaval and change after the reunification. He had been saving everything since 1936, and I wanted to throw everything away since 1989 and make room for new things. 14 bulk containers of 10m³ waste each were taken away from the old roofing business, and a fight ensued over each piece of content. At that time, I was partly right about clearing things out, but from today's perspective, I would like to have at least seven containers back because there were really good things in there. The good old tools, for example. Today, you buy a hammer from China, and on the first strike, the hammerhead flies off and smashes the cheap glasses of the person accross. Hammer and glasses are broken, and if you don't report it to the accident insurance right away, they can convict you in 30 years for visual impairment due to an intentional hammer blow. In the past, hammers stayed on the handle...mostly.

My grandpa above the rooftops

END OF A WAR

At this point, perhaps a bit about my grandfather's life. He passed away in 2011 at the age of 86. I am quite surprised with the amount of lessons on many levels I learned from my grandfather. As a mentor, he was unassuming – the good ones usually are. The beauty of it is that it didn't end with his death. Many little things I observed about him now live on in my life and reveal themselves as very useful little helpers. For example, a phrase with which he concluded a hopeless argument: „You're right, and I'll have my peace". I haven't witnessed a single conversation that continued after these words. The colliding opinions ebbed away in the sands of speech, and a silence settled in. With this magical trick, he had managed to drain the opponent of their energy at the last moment. Then again, he didn't engage in many arguments.

He was drafted into World War II at the age of 17 and didn't lose his composure even there. He ended up on the coast of France, beside an anti-aircraft gun. Being a flawless shooter, they quickly made him a gunner instead of a radio operator. One day, a British fighter plane flew toward him from the ocean and pulled up just before him along the steep coast. Helmar shot it down, the pilot ejected and landed with his parachute right in front of him. Helmar greeted him with the words, „You probably didn't see me, did you?" Then he kindly took the friendly British officer into custody.

Another story from this war is his last battle in the Ardennes in France, Hitler's last uprising that cost so many child soldiers their lives. My grandpa was in this battle. He entered with 103 soldiers and officers and told me it felt like bullets were coming from all directions. When it was all over, he found himself the sole unwounded person, with a severely wounded man in each arm. He had to leave one of them in the forest when he passed away. The other, an officer, he brought to his battalion, where he also died. Then they ordered him to place his friend on the pile with the others. Thus, he became the last survivor of his battalion and belonged to no one anymore. He decided that the war was over for him and began walking home. 1500 kilometers lay ahead of him, where the war was not yet over. He stole a horse and rode through the front lines, hiding in bomb craters from air raids. He said the safest thing was to lie in one of the first craters. They were deep enough and were never hit precisely the same again. And so, he ran and walked the race of his life until the Americans captured him on a farm, along with a few other scattered soldiers. With hands raised, they were led out of the stable and searched. When they felt something long and hard in his chest pocket, he said, „Harmonica, Harmonica", and the American occupier smiled and let him keep it. He described American captivity as very pleasant. He was assigned to the food distribution and was well taken care of, organized football games, and wrote home. His mother told him to stay in captivity because there was nothing to eat at home. And so, he waded through this shit war and eventually arrived back in his hometown of Cainsdorf.

Thankfully, he had luck; otherwise, I wouldn't exist. Thank you, my friend.

Soldier grandpa

THE FIRE

There also would be no Holly, or rather, not anymore if Opa hadn't dragged me out of his burning
house. A timber beam, inexplicably part of the chim-
ney, had been invisibly smoldering in the wall for
years. We called it the warm wall. One night, the fire
broke through the wall behind a floor-to-ceiling shoe
cabinet and set a firestorm in motion. Have you ever
seen shoes burn? It's not a burning; rather, it's a vol-
canic-like eruption of all the chemicals that were
melted into them.

I was a restless sleeper and spent that night in my
grandparents' bed. I woke them up with my tossing
and turning, which made them aware of the house
being up in flames. The bedroom was still smoke-
free when they snapped out of sleep, but the glass
door separating us from the fire in the house showed
bright red flames searching for more air to consume
and stuff to burn. In an attempt to escape through
the mix of thick smoke and flames they got out, but I
got lost. With too little oxygen and blinded by the
toxic fumes, I stood lost in the burning inferno. Milli-
seconds became endless moments, there was literally
no air to breathe and nowhere to go. I froze. Then a
hand came out of the dark, grabbed my arm and
pulled me out of hell. My grandpa had come back for
me. After I was safe, he ran in the streets and
screamed fire.

I was maybe seven or eight when all of this happened
and sat shivering in my lovely mother's arms who
had stayed downstairs that night. Eventually, the fire

department arrived and turned everything into a giant foamy bathtub, but the house remained standing. A bitter taste lingered after the flames were out and a black soup dripped from every wall that used to be our cozy home. When I think back to this night, I can still taste the smoke on my tongue.

Thank you for saving me again, my Opa, my old friend.

MY BALL COMES OFF

I spent a lot of time with my grandpa during my 12-year roofing career. Our joint company was growing, and we were gaining momentum when everything was about to change dramatically. It was in 1995, and I was around 25 years old. We were in the process of the construction of the new company building; the order books were full, and we had just taken out a bank loan of 660,000 West German Marks, a significant amount of money at the time. Everything felt like I could let the river flow upstream if I wanted to. I drove in my Toyota Land Cruiser convertible with my Bang&Olufsen mobile phone through the summer, thinking it couldn't get much better now. I still remember the spot on the road when it came through the phone... the diagnosis... testicular cancer. The world and the car came to a standstill. Me? Why me? The one who did everything right? My right testicle had noticeably enlarged, and I had finally mustered the courage to show it to the urologist and pick up some pills that would heal this. But no, cancer had come to visit, or to pick me up. In that moment, it felt like death, and all my values lost all meaning instantly.

The first question: „How long do I have left?" No answer. No one ever has an answer to those questions. Terrible. The second question: „How can I pretend that it's not that bad and tell my parents as gently as possible?" My father and I are very similar. Supposedly strong but internally very emotional in both directions. That's the most fertile ground for our common main fear: losing a child. It didn't take long, and he was on my urologist's phone. „Why cut off the testicle?" I heard them saying. "Oh, shit", I thought, "If he wants to cut it off right away, it must be really bad." He preferred to separate the source of death from my surviving body sooner rather than later, this Doctor B. Who was he anyway? How could he be so sure? But I had my super luck again. He was the best thing that could have happened to me in this chaos. What this man did for me in the next years is indescribable. He landed in the most intimate part of my life from one moment to the next and gracefully took on the role of the conductor. For a while, I became a passenger on my journey. The first big lesson of cancer had already begun. You had to trust.

As the first trust exercise, I was invited to trust someone with my life right away. In no time, I was on Doctor B's operating table. I was glad that he probably decided against all the rules of testicle removal to do an outpatient castration. This had the advantage that I didn't have to go to the hospital. I was allowed to keep my baseball cap on during the surgery for my spiritual protection. He knew immediately that it was important to me. It was the same cap I got from the father of the little boy at the Berlin Wall. It had possibly saved a life back then, so I thought it had magic in it. When they dragged me half-conscious into my grandparents' house after the surgery, my cap fell off. The doc stopped the transport and put the cap back on my head – a crucial moment that connected us. I was severely wounded, but my comrade didn't leave my important stuff behind. And so, I lay in my room, staring at the ceiling, hand on my half-empty ball sack, and was completely destroyed. This whole situation hit me at a point that you could call a bullseye. It tore me emotionally, physically, but also spiritually from my foundation. Cancer didn't fit into the life I had imagined. And who had done this to me? Spiritually immature, I tried to find the guilty one, but there was nowhere to put this, no one to put this on.

And the spot in my body where this hit me was also very hard to accept. My absolute favorite playground that I visited multiple times a day and never came back from disappointed. Another question came to my mind. Does it even still work? Oh shit! What if my last orgasm is now history? There was only one way to find out. Being reasonable was briefly considered and then dismissed. Carmen, my dear girlfriend at this time of my life, was against it. But who contradicts the last wish of a dying person? We did it, and I haven't forgotten to this day how happy I was when it came, the elixir of joy.

Doctor B, my urologist, won't forget it either. He had disappeared on a short vacation after my surgery. His substitute received a panicked call from me the next morning. When I woke up, my lower parts felt as if my removed testicle was back. But what was there instead was a massive bruise that had formed through my premature arousal test. The substitute doctor just shook his head when he saw it and ordered me „hands off". From now on I listened very carefully and was a good boy.

NO REST FOR THE WICKED

48 hours after all that, I was back in the office, standing behind the desk because sitting was still not possible. Healing had to take place after work, according to the German toughness. We were raised to believe that the body is only the means of transportation for the mind, carrying it from one job to another.

Well, I don't want to be too hard on myself. Sure, I worked way too much back then. Sometimes, I would glance over at my neighbor, the roofing material dealer, and if there was still light in his office, I would keep working. But during that time, I also tried to build something up. I was by no means capable of recognizing the value of quality idleness, let alone declaring it the highest state of being. Also, I believe it's rather difficult in Germany to slow down because no one else is doing it. You would not only feel like a weakling but would also feel alone. Today, fortunately, I am strong enough to sometimes pull through and rest when my body or mind wants to hit the sofa. But believe me, even if it doesn't look like it, it's still not quite easy, although I now recognize the value. It is a terrible belief system to prioritize work above well-being.

So, I hadn't learned much from cancer for the time being. Everything continued as planned, and healing would probably bring forgetfulness with it. But Mr. Cancer began to shape his powerful and inevitable transformation. I can't express how glad I am to be able to write about that time from the present moment. My Carmen stood by me like a rock, and after my initial strength, a flood of doubt overwhelmed me. No one could swear to me that it was gone. I started finding a long list of imaginary bumps and knots on my body. After the examination of my cut off testicle in the laboratory, the severity of this type of cancer was confirmed. I opted for chemotherapy. Surely, there must be a few readers who have been through something like this. But for the others, I can say this here: it's unbelievably awful. Firstly, you begin the targeted poisoning of any rapidly growing cells (meaning hair, nerves, liver and yes, cancers), and you are usually already seriously weakened. Then, and this is the truth, no one can tell you if it helps. But what is a fact is that you feel terribly ill: your inner self resists to the utmost, and in the end, you have a bald head. When I came out at the other side of this torture, my mental transformation began - surely, for the time being, subconsciously.

MY DAYS BACK THEN

So, I was in the process of establishing my company when the first doubts crept into the farthest corners of my thoughts. But as it is often the case in life, you cannot stop doing what you are currently engaged in. We plan for the long term, too much has to be created too quickly, with a lot of borrowed money. And just like that, we find ourselves in our golden cage of life. And as long as everything is enjoyable and goes according to plan, the engraved sign on the entrance door shines brightly.

Apart from my physical condition, I had no reason to question anything. One had to live capitalism before passing judgment on it. All I'm trying to say is that slowly, a slightly raised eyebrow appeared on my face. I remained diligent, built the company, constructed a house, had my grandparents move in, and renovated the old family home into a stylish three-family house. In the meantime, I earned my master's degree in roofing in evening school and attended my tumor check-ups. Economically, I had caught one of the most golden times that Germany had ever experienced. So, I returned almost every hard-earned penny to the bank and made extra payments like crazy, to pay off this rather large sum of money as soon as possible and gain back my freedom. The times where roofers did nothing in winter were over ever since the reunification. Thus, I broke with the tradition of winter vacations and traveled to a new country every summer to get a taste of the world.

There is much to tell about that too, but I would rather talk about my everyday life. This is how my days looked in the wild „Post-Cancer Capitalism Era". The alarm clock rang at 6:30 am (I've always thought we should all meet once a year, and everyone should be allowed to brutally beat their alarm clock). While brushing my teeth, I mentally organized my construction sites, assigned tools to the cars, and if I was lucky, the toothbrush didn't make me gag. Eating was out of the question. For years, I woke up with a nervous stomach. Then I showed up with theatrical ease and convincing morning freshness in front of my work crew and released my day plan for execution. They all went out, and I sank behind the desk with my coffee for a brief paperwork session. Then a construction site check. By 9 am, I had usually visited all the roofs we were working on and set everything in motion.

On the most challenging construction site, I usually worked alongside the others, always taking on the stuff nobody wanted to do. Later, I procured the material for the next day and usually ended up back at the company around 5 pm. By that time, everyone went home, and I went to meet with (potential) customers, estimated quotes, and wrote invoices. During that time, there hardly was a working day that was over before 8 pm. After work I went to see Carmen, and if she was already there, she had to listen to how my important day was, without me being interested in hers. We all worked so much in those days. But it was beautiful to see the fruits of our labor. Many houses in my city now began to showcase our style, adorned with beautiful roofs and turrets. I was proud to know that a piece of history was now being built by us.

One of my most beautiful works

BETTER OR NOT ?

Around 1995 the era of the amateur videographer arrived in the East. Everyone now had a pocket-sized video camera, filming everything extensively, and every experience was captured before it was truly lived. East Germans had no idea how to behave in front of a camera. We were trained to stay away from these things. So, whenever one of these devices was pointed at a group, you'd see people scatter, and whoever remained behaved and articulated themselves very strangely. This became especially clear to me in 2011 when I received the digitized video collection of my own recordings from my mother. But it is thanks to these Hollywood masterpieces that I now have some highly interesting scenes from our construction sites and general life during that time.

For example, I filmed the traditional roofing of an onion-domed tower with German natural slate. Every time I'm in Germany; I drive past that house and take pride in the clear German craftsmanship. I also have a recording of a trip with my hometown carnival club to the North Sea. You can see how clumsily East Germans tiptoed their way through the new West, rather adorable and awkward at the same time. The West Germans must have really thought we came from the moon. But the moon we came from seemed to be a planet of perpetual drunks who couldn't face reality. However, when I look at the faces of this group and mentally wander through the lives of each of these people, I have to say that the alcohol was somewhat justified. Many of them faced significant challenges with the arrival of this new era; some had to leave their homes to find work. Some were toppled by waves of bankruptcy beyond their control, and the rest somehow muddled through. Unfortunately, some did not.

If you were to ask me today whether people were better off before or after the reunification of Germany, my answer would probably be this: when you consider everything together - freedom to travel, health, prosperity or adversity, and quality of life - the needle of the „know-it-all-meter" would probably stay right in the middle. In my opinion, both socialism and capitalism, the old and the new Germany had their good and bad aspects. Until I think about laughter. This tips the scale toward the old days for sure. I am convinced that in the socialist East, people laughed more warmly, carefree, and maybe most importantly, more often. I really miss that funny smile in the eyes of our nation.

TURNING AROUND

Perhaps you have already wondered why there are only very few years mentioned here. Over time, I've lost my connection to numbers and am not very interested in finding it again. Numerical life seems quite disjointed to me, and I am often annoyed when a story dies because of the correct year. You all know when roughly all of this happened. I do too: in the past, of course. In the past, we worked, worked some more, and the cars became bigger and more beautiful.

The display of prosperity slowly sneaked its way into existence, while we also tried to deny it.

People are not made for a lot of money. There is an automatic detachment from others. Here you can argue (philosophize) whether it is intentional or not, but the result is always the same. One simply does not stop acquiring things and securing one's flock, not just to ensure their safety, but to enlarge the herd. I really have no problem with people who work hard and are dedicated, earning a lot of money. The problem for me is that hardly anyone manages to do this without doing it over the backs or behind the backs of others. And if it's not stolen from people, nature has to pay for it. Even though none of us like to hear or admit it, we all know it.

And so, we lived abundantly but always with a beautiful spoonful of guilt. Our children were already so well provided for, that there might be nothing left for the grandchildren.

There are only a few events that can throw us out of a well-functioning, constantly growing life enterprise. One of the things that can happen is that the partner you „love" simply leaves, due to neglect. This usually happens completely unexpectedly, and the luster of everything that was achieved immediately fades. Or, what also can change things is an illness that provides a reality check, bringing the essence of life back into focus. But if things are going smoothly, hardly anyone would want to change. If you're not fired, usually nothing fires...

For me, it was „love" that moved out and moved in with my 'best friend'. It was completely incomprehensible to me how one could leave such a dynamic person like me, and then for someone like him - someone I actually liked. I was completely devastated. And so, the thinking processes began, which were so important to explore the only true rhythm of my own life. The pain, often referred to by me as the engine of personal evolution, brought my heart and brain to a standstill in a kind of wakeful coma. But I didn't see anything yet. Only more and more things came to light that were uncomfortable. I began to feel uncomfortable, and the feelings began to grow. But where to go? The word „away" came up every now and then.

So, there it was, the big inventory after the first phase of life where conscious decisions had been made. And what a mess it was. Let me tell you how the beginning of my turning point felt. I was on the way 'back to myself'.

FUTURE AND THE PAST

I felt shitty, really shitty... But what was the situation, exactly? We Germans are good at thinking ahead and reflecting on the past, but when it comes to the present, we're a bit stuck. So, let me describe the whole thing with two boxes: the future on the right and the past on the left, as a nice visual example. I'll start with the future because at the time, I was more concerned about that. The business was doing well, the money was rolling in, but the effort to keep it that way seemed to be enormous. In Germany, it's either full throttle all the time, or you fall behind. But which hunter can run through the forest like a wild boar without ever taking a breather? Who does that? At some point you are bound to hit a tree and crash. I always wondered if society had no interest in time at all.

Well... the desire to keep pushing that gigantic mountain of work was pretty much zero. People weren't that cheerful during this period either because everyone was busy, and there really was no time for anything else. On top of that, I wouldn't find a woman as beautiful as Carmen, so to summarize: all hope was lost, everything was crap, and I also realized how messed up I was. Any chance of changing something immediately faded because of the system I had built for myself, a common situation during this time for many people. Contracts with customers, banks, and insurances ended up becoming guarantee certificates, which could only be canceled after a certain period if the deficiency was proven, and that speculative period ended earlier than the investment allowance repayment could have been... Did you notice how your forehead just furrowed? Exactly.

The future was too hopeless to cut ties quickly. And did I even really want to do that? I already knew that if I started dismantling the whole thing, the money would stop immediately. I was scared of that. Talking about changing your life is one thing, but actually doing it... a whole different story. Leaving everything as it was wasn't an option either, which brings us to the box of the past. There was certainly more stability in this box. If I continued to make an effort, everything would go as planned until my 68th birthday. A few highs and lows, but the definite guarantee of a rather moderate life. But when I looked back from the future, from my 68 year old self, hardly anyone had appeared in all these years who had truly inspired me or surprised me in any way. Like I said, we Germans are good at looking at the future and the past, even some weird combination of it, but the present is a field unknown to us.

I was alive, but not at the wheel, and I also felt I was becoming boring. It was like the funeral of spontaneity. So, continuing from this perspective wasn't really going forward either.

VEGETATIVE STATE

You already notice that the decision-making process revolved exclusively around my job. So, even while writing this, it becomes clear to me once more that back then everything really revolved around work. Everything was measured by it, it was constantly talked about, and everything, yes everything, was set up around it. I felt like I was in an invisible, very comfortable prison. The house was new, the TV large, a Gibson Les Paul on the wall (which I couldn't play), the accounts and hiding places for money were full and „healthy".

My mental gaze began to wander whenever the heartache, in which I am, incidentally, the undefeated world champion, allowed a glimmer of light. It's embarrassing how, in such affluence, we manage to feel uncomfortable, thinking that the world has us by the neck. No matter how much effort we put into it, we damn well can't find that satisfied feeling we're all looking for. But if we can't manage to take the steps that finally let us relax with a rational mindset, then there must inevitably be another way of thinking that will lead us to satisfaction. A way of living or feeling that doesn't, or not only, comes from the head. But where has that carefree attitude in well-provided circumstances gone? Where was the understanding to recognize that everything was actually good?

I can only say it like this. Now, looking back on those old „fat days", a crucial element was missing that would have restored the balance. A force that was lost through time-consuming progress and our television and news lifestyle. The development of our spiritual side. This was brutally neglected, not promoted or respected socially, and was too risky because it is not tangible... at least not with the mind alone.

Upon entering the working world of full-throttle capitalism, it was considered rather weak to deal with one's inner circus. Actually, no attention whatsoever was given to the whole thing. So it was completely absent and maybe not even missed for that reason. I was quite speechless during that time about what had become of me and us. A vegetative state is truly a good term for it. And who wouldn't want to wake up from such a stupor? What if you are allowed to move, to stretch? Maybe the life police aren't paying attention for a moment, and you can steal back a bit of craziness. I had few answers and plenty of questions...

And again, people entered my life who were supposed to bring about significant changes. People who unlocked doors. People who can twist signposts. People who tinker with your life and thereby refine their own...

PUSHED OFF THE CLIFF

Kirsten, for example. In the midst of this chaos, I called her 'privately' for the first time. We knew each other from the business world and from a mini-flirt during a bank appointment. Kirsten sold money for the bank, and I bought it. What she didn't know back then was that in the future she would be paying off this loan with me, the very one she had just sold to me and my future ex with her charming smile. Back then, Kirsten was still in a relationship, and so was I, but we had noticed each other. Later, when we were both semi-single, we found each other again. She had the most beautiful telephone voice in the world. I actually addressed her as 'Frau Lorenz' quite often and always came up with new questions to make her answers nice and long. At some point during this turbulent time of change, we met at the fountain in front of the Gewandhaus in Zwickau, briefly attempted to have a drink, and then withdrew to her chamber. What I didn't know was that Kirsten had been warned by another ex-girlfriend about what kind of a rogue I was. But I had already won her heart. However, everything didn't look so good. Kirsten had not only gone through a very tough time in her previous relationship but also had a heart-wrenching time ahead. Her father, an exceptionally positive, popular, and incredibly close person, was very, very ill, fatally ill. How she managed to shower me with so much love during that time and repeatedly listen to my trivialities is a monumental testament to her seemingly endless kindness.

I – and that was all that mattered to me at that time – actually wanted to either leave or get back together with my ex. And so, the lovely Kirsten ended up in a Bermuda Triangle between the tragedy in her family, the attempts to reconcile me with my former partner, and her love for me, a bewildered charmer seeking salvation in the final escape. Great vision for everyone involved. But precisely during this time when we, as small individuals, had to make so many significant decisions, she was an enchantingly strong friend to me. My person who could hold me and protect me from going crazy. We spent endless nights talking, drinking red wine, holding each other. During these nights it became increasingly clear that I would have to change my territory. But was that even possible? And what about Kirsten? She couldn't leave, absolutely not.

The final blow to my previous commercial life came from another 'friend'. He had asked me for money to save his company. Many of us small business owners were struggling with unpaid invoices at that time, and if you couldn't compensate for this by yourself, health insurance agencies and tax offices closed you down. So, I gave him the money to save his ass. But I took collateral for it. One of his trucks. My 'friend' ended up not being able to raise the money again. Instead, out of shame he started telling the business world that I had damaged his truck and that that was the reason why he had to close down. When this information finally reached me, the business rumor mill was already in full swing, and now it was being said that my company was also bankrupt. As a result, I lost a massive number of customers at that time, but the dagger in the heart was much worse. I had helped him in a hopeless situation and now stood defenseless under a brutal surprise attack.

I had nothing to counter with. I was mentally bankrupt. This event finally pushed me over the edge. I collapsed. And of course, immediately called my guardian angel, who was on permanent duty to revive me. We met promptly at „1470", a small, quaint pub in Zwickau. There, we cried so much together that the waiter asked if he should get more tissues because the house reserves were depleted. We said "yes, please," and a new box appeared. What became clear in that key moment was that I really had to get moving. A new life journey began. There was simply no reason to continue like this. But there was also no vision. There was only a completely torn soul that began to drag itself away from the battlefield, with the equally tearing guilt of leaving Kirsten behind. But the queen of crisis management sent me off... Her strength is indescribable to this day.

My Kirsten (Kiki)

FALLING FREE

The free fall, while the rest of my surroundings clung to everything, really felt like falling, not at all liberating. But that was just how it had to be now. And what was I actually risking? Even this answer was no longer relevant. I had to gain a bird's-eye view at any cost. As a German, I was cautious enough to keep every back door wide open. Even if this step of 'getting out' seemed very courageous and risky to almost everyone, it felt like others risked much more than me. It would have been risky to leave everything as it was. That was way more dangerous than my step. For me, my entire life was at stake back then. So, I had to set myself in motion. But where to?

Jack London luckily had answered that question for me. This magical writer had told me about a distant land in his book 'The Call of the Wild', a land which was tucked away somewhere in the upper left corner of the world map. The mighty Yukon magically sent me a feeling that the North liked me. The wildness gave me the impression that the little boy would be well placed there to learn how to float in the river of time. Perhaps the North could breathe into me what I should do with the rest of my life. And so, the Yukon River itself had already begun to attract me in its indescribable way. An inevitable force that I would later experience in all its mystique.

One of my best friends from that time was the first to learn about my plan to feel out a real Canadian adventure and paddle down the Yukon... alone. He even decided, because I was quite shaky, to accompany me with his entire family to Canada to send me off. And so, I left my job, kissed the weeping Kirsten goodbye, and flew to British Columbia for the first big trip of my own life, accompanied by my best friend. There, after a two week vacation, we planned to part ways, and I would head north. And so, we paddled with boats across much too stormy lakes, walked through the largest forests in the world, and drank bad beer. A lot of it. Alcohol seemed a good friend in these times. Of course, also in other times, but during those weeks in Canada, no parasites could really settle in me. During long nights, we often noticed that we had to drag occasional guest drinkers from our fires long before we were done with our own intoxication. Once, a newly arrived Taiwanese left our fire only to vomit a minute later into his fully occupied large family tent. When the headlamps in his bush hotel turned on, my friend and I enjoyed the funniest shadow puppet performance that was globally shown on that crazy day.

But of course, I was scared. The separation from the 'shoulder to lean on' was imminent, and soon I would be standing by the road with only my backpack and myself. I was emotionally in rough shape, and the step into „aloneness" was really scary.

VISITING MY SLEEPING HALF

I still see them driving away in their Canadian rental car. As my friends disappeared on the horizon, I stuck my first free thumb into the wind. This little Erzgebirge guy hitchhiked through the Rockies. I'll spare you the long descriptions of the people I met and tell you how I felt instead. First of all, pretty wild. Wearing my self-sewn leather pants, a hat, and with a knife on my belt, I looked like I had fallen out of a Western movie. Canadians can always immediately recognize Germans because we always dress up as adventurers, while a note from our international health insurance always hangs out of our back pocket. They were all kind to me here in the Wild West. And even though I know today that the percentage of assholes in the world is the same everywhere, I really liked the positive greeting ritual of „How are you?".

As a novice in the Wild West, you start answering the question „How are you?" in detail, which no one truly cares about. It's just a „Good to see you" in disguise. But that was already a fantastic start. Someone encountered you without reservation, invitingly, and without business thoughts and was happy to see you.

And so, I moved towards Whitehorse, the starting point of my river journey. At night, I always had the wildest dreams. They were not beautiful, and mostly filled with heartache, fear, or guilt, but at least the view was different when I woke up. And so, I pulled myself through each day and enjoyed the freedom to try things out. Looking back at my former self today, at how disheveled, hurt, and confused I was, I know that the days were not easy. But I know that I had done something to make them better.

On my way to the „upper left of the world", I came across a village of the indigenous people of this country. I can no longer use the word „Indian" morally when talking about my friends. They're not from India at all. They were only called that because a Portuguese sailor got lost, and the white man was later too proud to admit the mistake. In any case, there I entered my first earth house. A round, large room under the forest floor with a wooden roof, which, in turn, was covered with earth. When I first sat down in there, my hair stood on end. I felt, as if struck by lightning, how intimately these people were connected to their environment. And as great as this impression was, my inner self immediately harmonized synchronously with this way of life. It was nothing that wasn't already in me; it was just revived with brute force. It felt as if a world that had moved parallel to me for a while was now reconnecting inseparably with my existence. I was touched and sat for a long time with the first cautious feeling of happiness in the wonderfully air-conditioned cave. There, I also received the first Canadian sage as a gift. A scent that is my absolute undisputed favorite smoke. I was told that with it, one can shed the old and invite good spirits into one's life. And to this day, I smudge everything important in my life with this sweet miracle.

But what this moment brought me above all was the long overdue reunion with my spiritual life. The counterpart to our scientifically explainable life. Such an important part of our existence, without which we can never find peace. But I had touched it again, the pleasant feeling that there is something in me that only concerns me. Something so individual and alive that its care and attention had to be a main part of my healing. Our very personal mystical connection to everything around us is, for me, one of the most neglected teachings in our industrial societies to this day. However, pausing and synchronizing with life and living beings around you is based on these very rites. More than ever, it is existential to take care of our spiritual body. And it's beautiful too.

ON MY WAY NORTH

The journey north was surely worth covering a book in itself. But because I want to share so many things with you, I'll limit myself to my personal favorite memories. One of them is that during a Greyhound bus ride, I met a young person traveling with a huge pile of loose sheets of paper. When Curtis - that was his name - explained to me that he was writing a hiking book about the Yukon, containing all his hikes, maps, and favorite spots, I was very impressed. I had encountered an actual book writer, and I genuinely thought, „Is he allowed to do that?" Yes, I was really that stiff. Until then, I thought not just anyone could write a book about anything. Didn't you have to study something like book writing? But Curtis just did it. In fact he wasn't an actual book writer; actually, he was a young gardener, evidently writing a book. It was in that very moment that I first understood that anyone could do anything, and there was no moral police constantly watching to ensure that you only did what you were 'qualified' for. Curtis with his book gave me the permission to try things out, things in which I might find myself. Somehow, I wasn't aware previously of this freedom. And because this bus ride was 20 years ago, and I'm already quite old now, I can tell you that his book became a hit. If you go to Yukon bookstores today, Curtis is on the top shelf. Every time I see it, I grin because I see a piece of my history.

And the second and perhaps even more important story is that of my first travel guitar. It wasn't really my first. I had received one as a kid from my dad. But at that time, I wasn't ripe for it and undid the strings and went fishing with it. But the second little companion came from German immigrants on my way north. They had found the little guitar in the attic of their newly purchased house. It was a 3/4 Marlin with nylon strings, which I replaced with steel strings, immediately leading to the deformation of the little old lady. But regardless, it sounded better, and I had no clue anyway. I couldn't even dream of the stories that this little gem would trigger. I noticed during the first steps we took together that it was an intense companion. Since I could hardly play back then, it was more like a piece of furniture that I carried around, but the impact was tremendous on so many levels. Conversations started faster, and cars stopped when you stood in the rain. Invitations followed, and often, very often, plucking a single string could keep loneliness at bay, which haunts you when traveling solo.

The two of us looked very sweet together, so free and young on the roadside. This guitar took me to new places, introduced me to people, and began to write my story. My first E-minor sounded amazingly cool, and the first shreds of „Rockin' in the free world" or „Losing my religion" became my new companions. Other people with instruments now became my friends and mentors. But more than the music itself, it was the presence of the 'Little One' that mattered. When it hummed its vibrations through my body, it gave me support to explore new terrain. And often, it patiently listened to my sobbing when my world collapsed again and again. This musical upgrade brought not only more inner peace, new friends, and an endless learning task; it also took me to the wildest places that were still in my future back then. For example, it started playing alone when I stood years later at Hierve el Agua in Oaxaca, Mexico. When the strong wind began to resonate all the strings simultaneously by itself, I almost fell off this holy mountain. It also took me to a basement in Aberdeen, Washington, owned by a friend of Kurt Cobain. Nirvana had started here, and much stuff from that time was still there. My host signed my guitar with „Kurt's friend" and gave me an old effects pedal from the grunge master, which I treated like treasure. Later, I gifted the pedal to the Nirvana cover band „April Hate" in Montreal, and they still rock with it to this day. And who would have thought that 20 years later, Nirvana's tour cellist Lori Goldstone from the „MTV unplugged session" would play on my record „Casanova", and Dave Grohl has a copy of my „Aura Borealis" CD. Yes, I know... It's all hardly believable, but I haven't lied.

When you know the first three chords, the campfires aren't so lonely anymore. I still have the good wandering-man guitar today, but it's in a plastic bag. It has been murdered. I had lent it to a temporary neighbor who was mentally unstable, and I thought it would help because he was sad and lonely. At some point, it ended up in his crosshairs and he destroyed it and returned to me as a woodpile in a bag. I kept it because I think its presence will find its way into one of my art installations some day. We still have a joint performance ahead of us, maybe our biggest one ever.

I'll keep you posted.

The Curtis book

My traveling guitar

SKAGWAY

To travel down the Yukon, one had to first journey all the way up north. Since I embarked on the Klondike Gold Rush about 100 years too late, at least I knew the way. Most of the somewhat over-optimistic gold seekers back then arrived by ship through the Inside Passage along the Canadian West coast to land in Skagway, Alaska. There, they tried to gather the remaining equipment to then conquer the 53-kilometer-long „Chilkoot Trail" with all their belongings to reach Canada. If they hadn't died by then, they were forced to handcraft a wooden boat, wait for the ice to break on the lake, and then row 700 kilometers down the Yukon River to Dawson. And that's where the real adventure began.

It all sounded very far out, but in a trip-descriptive picture book, I had closely examined the photos. It showed completely ordinary people, and I was still in good shape from GDR competitive sports and high-performance roofing. At least now there were canoes, so I didn't have to carve a boat.

And so, my journey to Skagway began at the port of Prince Rupert. I bought a ticket for the ship heading north. It already sounded a lot like Huckleberry Finn with a touch of Grizzly Adams on the way to Jack London. And because I had a cheap ticket, I was allowed to take a berth on the open upper deck. During the days, I spent my time observing the mountains and glaciers passing by from the safety of my sleeping bag. During this departure, which was as exciting for me as the Titanic leaving port, I kept thinking about the people from 100 years ago who didn't even have a return ticket. It seemed unimaginably adventurous and put into perspective what I was currently up to. The pioneers had no idea where their food, medicine, or ammunition would come from but traveled to the freezer of the world with unwavering confidence. Compared to these fighters and heroines, I was a softie in brand-name shoes. And yet, mentally, I was on the edge of my capacity to undertake such a journey and proud to have raised the anchor. Yes, I was proud, and I now let the wind hit my face. Wait a moment, sunscreen first. There we go. Now.

After a magnificent bluewater journey with whales and dolphins, I checked into the Golden North Hotel in Skagway. Like something out of a movie, this place on the Main Street of this frontier town wasn't a movie set. What stood here was the real deal. Back then, the exhausted souls leaned against these spruce shacks and hoped to get a whiskey to keep standing. This was where 21-year-old Jack London had passed through. And now, Holly stared out the window and would later have a bath in the magnificent lion-footed tub. And because I had to prove this photographically later, I started balancing my camera on a stack of towels. Tub filled, naked with a hat, I pressed the self-timer, and climbed into the tub. As I tried to position myself and form a grin, I realized through shocking pain that I should have checked the water temperature. But being a disciplined German, you don't waste a shot and wait for the camera to flash. The better picture would have been me fleeing from the tub attempting to put out the fire on my skin. There he was again, the man from the mountains, red as a lobster and ready for a calming whiskey. Man, did I have a lot to learn.

On the ship to Alaska

Skagway

Golden North Hotel

THE CHILKOOT TRAIL

There it was, the famous „Chilkoot Trail" over the pass to Canada. In Skagway, many historical photos from the days of the Gold Rush awaited my study. Whenever I'm at historically significant places, I want to touch and see everything, awakening the spirits that journeyed there before me – I had now become one of them. So there I stood, on the street where Soapy Smith had his shootout with the sheriff and died. I walked on the path where Jack London collected impressions for his books and passed through the bottleneck where every good-time girl, every banker, every horse, and every dog team had to go on their way to the Klondike. They were all here, and many saw the sea for the last time in their lives, especially the horses. None of them made it through the trail, which is why a considerable stretch of the trail is called the „Dead Horse Trail". Thousands of our loyal companions froze, were eaten, or simply collapsed under their load. Later, I would find many of their bones. But to get there I had to take my first steps into the unknown. I was a bit scared but thought the hiking was manageable. First through the jungle-like coastal rainforest, then up the 45-degree steep 'Golden Stairs', and finally on high-alpine flower meadows to Lake Bennett. I didn't even have much luggage. Compared to me, the gold prospectors had to drag a ton of provisions and equipment. The Canadians wouldn't let them in otherwise, due to famine and such. That's why my hiking ancestors made the trail up to 40 times. So it must be possible that the defending vice-champion of Nordic combined skiing might make it up there somehow. But because I'm Holly, everything was going to be different again.

After the first miles through the wonderfully dense wet rainforest and dozens of bear tracks, I arrived at „Finnegan's Point" and met with great relief an Austrian trio consisting of a 60-year-old married couple and their equally ancient friend (back then, I thought that was old; this looks considerably different today). The age of my newfound friends was particularly relaxing for me because now I thought, if they can make it up there, I can smell the flowers. We decided to set up our camp together in the next base in Canyon City, and I walked ahead. There was an old log cabin with a stove, which I had already brought to a glow when they arrived quite exhausted. I was the king. The friend of the couple thanked me extensively for the warmth and told me about her fear of the next 2 days. I gave her the courage I didn't have and handed her one of my sugar tablets, which I slipped to her as a super-hiking-energy tablet. She was reassured, and I became her tour guide in case she fell behind. In my heart, I was really glad to be able to help her. Friendship had often been tested to the breaking point on this trail, yet it was always the reason for less pain and good progress. We bolstered each other up. The old man of the group, an alpine guru with a thick Austrian accent, proudly revealed a bottle of „Obstler" (fruit schnapps). My eyes lit up like gold since I hadn't added the weight of such medicine to my load. He gave a little speech about the usefulness of the bottle and that he never hiked

anywhere without one. Then he led it ceremoniously
to his mouth. After his first sip, I thought I would get
the vessel to lighten its load a bit, but I witnessed an
outburst of rage in Austrian dialect. It sounded very
threatening, and the cabin suddenly felt small, and I
looked toward the door. After what seemed to be an
eternity he finally calmed down and it turned out that
his friends, who gave him the bottle, had played a
prank on him and filled it with water. He never for-
gave them. I witnessed a friendship burial in Alpine
style. I wouldn't have wanted to be in the shoes of
his ex-buddies when they returned home, and I
found it pretty crappy myself. I also didn't have any
schnapps because of the darn idiots. Well, now it was
time to sleep. What could possibly happen? We bed-
ded ourselves in sleeping bags on the ground of our
little cute cabin and dreamt, surrounded by old spirits.

Shortly after drifting off, a terrifying scream sounded
next to my ear. You wouldn't believe how quickly
you can stand up with a sleeping bag. The single lady
of the group sat up like a pole in her sleeping bag and
screamed in full panic: „Muuuus". I knew the word
from English as moose. I began to dive for the head-
lamp, assuming a moose had broken into the cabin.
Now we had a collective panic because she didn't
stop screaming, and I tried to find this giant animal.
No one was there. And so I learned, after all the
lights came on, that „Muuuus" in Austrian slang
means 'mouse' and she had a few of them in her
sleeping bag. That would have been another wonderful opportunity to have schnapps, when we finally

got the mice out. We layed down again, and our little friends immediately came back to visit again. Many of them, quite a lot. Perhaps that's why the sign outside said 'don't sleep in the cabin.' We didn't. No one closed an eye.

CAMP BEFORE THE SUMMIT

The next section was indeed a beautiful hike, with enough breaks to compensate for the sleepless night. The historically rich path along the creek was dotted with abandoned belongings from the last century, each piece telling a story. I could align my always-commentating mind well with my steps and felt quite comfortable. I must have dawdled a bit when I wandered off and didn't immediately find the path again after a somewhat tangled section. In „real time" it was maybe only seconds in which I was lost, but my blood boiled immediately, and I began to pay close attention to where I was going. Man, you just really don't want to get lost out there. This mini-shock was a wake-up call for my inner GPS and would keep me on the right trails for many years.

Sheep Camp was the goal of the day, and the camp where the only picture of Jack London's journey was taken. I found the spot where my favorite romanticist stood back then, and my heart was really, really big. I still enjoy following my heroes and seeing a bit of the world through their eyes. Jack was here, and I was here.

My Austrians also arrived well, and so we all went to bed after the park ranger informed us about the bear situation in the camp. Bears were there but generally caused no trouble. I was too tired to be afraid and fell asleep, the steep ascent to the golden stairs before my fading eyes. The next morning, I woke up with knee pain. Not bad, but not pleasant either. Because I always feel nauseous in the morning, I didn't need to cook anything and said goodbye to my fellow hikers, setting off. It was thick fog. Then, slowly, as I climbed higher, the mist transformed into zero-degree rain. Creepy, but because it was so strenuous and exciting, I felt warm and sang to myself. I enjoyed my adventurous spirit and my early start, which gave me plenty of time to make it over the pass to Happy Camp when suddenly a figure appeared behind me. Out of the rain, a tall man stomped. Wearing a wool sweater, an open leather coat, and also holding an open bottle of rum. He walked by like a ghost through the fog. He had zero equipment with him and disappeared as quickly as he had startled me. The appearance of this man made me think again about how little I actually trusted myself. I was fully equipped, well-shod, had food with me, and still felt nervous. And this pirate strolled the Chilkoot with a bottle? But everything would turn out differently.

Sheep Camp

LIVE HANGING BY A HAIR

As I slid over the first slippery stones of the 45-degree steep „Golden Stairs", the snowstorm began. Yes, a snowstorm in August. A 45-degree slope means one meter forward is one meter upward. Often crawling on all fours, I thought of the senior lady behind me, probably taking her dextrose energy pill. She would be needing it. On a nice day, all of this would have been funny, but the weather chilled me down and then thoroughly beat me up. Nothing was visible, but the valley was so narrow that even I couldn't get lost.

When I reached the pass at the top, everything was white - as in, I was unable to distinguish anything from anything - and I just wanted to quickly get down the other side, hoping to get out of this mess. Stopping was not an option. I was wet, cold, and miserable when, right in front of me, a lady appeared. She wore a red snowsuit and asked me, while my jaw dropped to my shoes, „Do you want a hot chocolate?"

My world stopped, and I wanted to pinch her to check if she was real. Perhaps she was just a ghostly friend of the Rum Pirate I had seen before. But she was very real and explained that there was a bad weather warning, and she was dropped off by the Canadian Rangers by helicopter to watch over us.

I joyfully followed her into a small shelter and slurped the hot brown milk. It was warm, and my body melted with enjoyment into the chair. She asked me what I knew about the other hikers, so I told her what I knew and asked back if the foggy man also had received hot chocolate. She looked at me stunned and replied that no one had passed by in the last 2 hours. With horror, both of us realized that the ghost was still out there. But how could I have overlooked him, where was he?

I put on my wet gear again, and we clattered down the slushy trail. For the first time, I understood how tough the Chilkoot could be and how closely life and death were intertwined here a hundred years ago. No sign of our hiker. She then told me about a small rock ledge where gold prospectors left things that proved useless for further travel. We crawled along the small edges, winding around a corner. Not far, but invisible from the main trail. At the end of this small traverse amidst Gold Rush remnants, he sat. Leaned against a rock wall and was unresponsive. We couldn't even get a name out of his deeply chilled soul, so we started pushing and pulling the wet sack over the snow. She in front, me behind. All the way to the little cabin. I just thought, „What the heck is going on here again?" and almost had a grin if it hadn't been so serious. The boy didn't look good, and I remembered a photo in my hometown. It hangs in a pub, the „Prijut". A picture of a frozen person, with my GDR mountaineering friends 'Lutz and Co.' climbing past a dead body on their way to the peak of the Elbrus. It was only 1000 and a few crushed meters high, but this gentleman would have looked moldy by spring too.

When we finally had him in the cabin, he didn't get chocolate but a super professional hypothermia rescue from the guardian angel. First, we undressed him, after which she administered some medicine, and an hour later, a helicopter flew him out. I was glad to have been in the right place at the right time, and the park ranger and I celebrated the rescue, while my thoughts circled around where the rum did end up. It stayed somewhere out there, along with the other witnesses of this violent mountain ridge on the edge of Canada. We then talked about the other upcoming hikers, and my Austrian friend came to mind again. I warmed up a bit more and descended down the Golden Stairs again to meet them. When I found them, I took my friends' backpack and made my second ascent, and everyone arrived safely. I must have been quite full of adrenaline because I said goodbye after another warm-up to reach my night camp in the somewhat distant Happy Camp. My older friend hugged me warmly because we knew we would lose sight of each other now, and our lives would go their own ways again. What we didn't anticipate at that time was that a few years later, I would climb the Inca Trail to Machu Picchu with her daughter. The world is small in the mountains.

When I arrived completely exhausted at the Happy Camp, I wasn't happy at all and very alone. No stove and not a piece of wood up there. As soon as I stopped, I started to shake. So I kept going but realized I wouldn't get far. After a few agonizing contemplative minutes, I decided to ignore the signs of my exhausted body and hike down to the valley, at least to get out of the crappy weather. Getting to the next camp was more of an illusion. I got out of the weather, but I couldn't stop anymore. I was too weak to set up a tent and too cold to sleep without one. It got dark, and in delirium, I wandered quite lost and far beyond my performance limit down the muddy trail into the valley. The damn hut would come at some point. And it did. When I opened the door, a scene unfolded like in a wilderness movie. The hut was packed, the stove glowed, and someone read a poem by Robert Service (a legendary northern poet). I must have looked pretty terrible as I hung in that door frame like that. The poetry stopped immediately, someone took my backpack off, someone gave me a warm rum, and I would have loved to pee for joy when they made room for me at the stove. I probably cried a bit at first. They couldn't believe where I had just come from. They knew about the weather warning and had all hidden in the hut. Everyone else had stayed on the other side of the pass. Only little Holly strolled through the mud storm to the little hut after climbing the „Golden Stairs" twice. I didn't witness the end of the cup of rum, fell asleep, and stayed there an extra day. The next morning, I dragged my blistered feet and lame bones to the end of the trail on the tracks of the old Bennett railway. Holy shit, what a trip. Just imagining in admiration of the old stampeders who now had to go back and get the next load of their freight. They were really made of a different kind of wood than the little „Driftwood Lolly". But at least I had helped to save a life.

„The Golden stairs" 1897

The Chilkoot Pass

THE ROBBERY

I rested in the hostel in Skagway after this taxing journey like a good German. I took an entire afternoon off and then headed straight to Whitehorse. There, at the end of Lake Laberge, the mighty Yukon River begins. Whitehorse is also the last city for several hundreds of kilometers where you can get provisions and equipment. Although there is a small store in Carmacks directly by the river and somewhere further down the river a family in the forest, you really have to plan ahead for the approximately 600 kilometers. The idea that you simply can't get anything out there is quite unsettling. In my home country, you can't go 10 kilometers without running into a wiener stand, and if your canoe goes missing here, you're in deep trouble. These facts brought my attention to the master level. Get your shit together, cause no one else will do it. No lawyers, no phone, no rescue helicopters, and when I would loudly scream for mommy, only an echo would come back.

So, first of all, I bought plenty of noodles. With noodles, I could paddle to the ends of the earth. And with cheese and salami... and with beer. At least I didn't have to carry it on my back. I want to apologize that in this book, I celebrate alcohol so much as a necessity and a psychotherapist. Of course I only learned later in life that this doesn't really work. But in this book, I'm still young, and I needed my beer. So, for the first time in my life, I started thinking two or three weeks ahead about what I might still have to nibble on, on the last day. Back then, I still thought that adventurers would die as soon as the food ran out. Today, I know that one can go for up to 48 days without food if one really has to. Such situations hardly ever happen, but it's good to know that you won't immediately be a dead man, just a hungry one. But I didn't want to starve, so I bought a few extra noodles. And a pack of eggs.

During these days, my base camp was at a campground near Whitehorse by the river. In the evenings, I would sometimes go to the village saloon to pick the brains of the locals and learn more about my journey through the wilderness. And then two things happened at once.

Firstly, I carelessly left one of my most important bags hanging on a tree in front of my tent. When I returned to my camp, it was gone, and I immediately had to start grieving the loss of my favorite knife, my smudging sage, all my medicine, and a spirit necklace. All these things were very important to me, and the surprise that someone would steal in the forest made me even more sad.

Secondly, in the saloon, I learned that a canoeist from The Netherlands had drowned in Lake Laberge. The wind on the lake can be really tricky, and everyone advised against paddling out in the open canoe in the next few days. When the Dutchman's equipment was found on shore, I was convinced that I had to start the journey below the lake to avoid the same fate. The river itself is supposed to be very calm, but I decided to hitchhike to Carmacks and rent a boat there. In any case, I now definitely had enough noodles to get me all the way to the Bering Sea.

DOWN THE RIVER WITH A KITCHEN KNIFE

So, I hitchhiked with all my provisions to Carmacks, had a canoe brought there, and tried to organize myself. With my tent on the Yukon's shore, I became neighbors with a young couple from whom I was about to learn to 'simply stand still', to pause. Growing up, I somehow always found myself on the run. In a peculiar way – that accompanies me to this day – that no matter our situation, we just cannot linger. My instinct told me to pack up quickly and go. However, the young couple, a beautiful Argentine woman and a Canadian man, lounged so wonderfully that I allowed myself to relax for three days and took it easy. It was delightful, just watching the river as it began to slowly rearrange my life. A feeling started to emerge that the river of life had something to do with the water in front of me. That the Yukon was just there, and I could just be there too. It began a time when my self-imagined life police, who looked over my shoulder and guilt tripped me with tireless precision, took small breaks. Very small breaks... but from these breaks, cute happy little moments emerged, in which you could sense the feeling that my hands were slowly reaching for the steering wheel of my own life.

On the third day, I was ready to entrust myself to the giant river. Unfortunately, a native took my spare knife home with him during the nighttime farewell party, what made me very sad. Now I know that the white men in the past took everything from them, including their children. My Winnetou romanticism quickly faded after learning the historical facts, and today I have the utmost respect for how the northern tribes deal with the past after all the attempts to exterminate them. But they survived and are getting stronger and I am fortunate and honored to call some of them my friends. Friends who were separated from their mothers as children, whose hair was cut, and whose language forbidden. Many of them simply disappeared. Today, these same tribes stand on the front lines to defend our ecosystem because they know how closely we are all connected to it. Up here, for over 12,000 years, people have lived with the cycles of nature without getting anything from the outside. The knowledge of indigenous people is just as valuable as the insights of our science. My instinctive thinking and my values are very similar to their way of living. No one taught me that. I was always connected with my environment and will remain so beyond my death because it is the most important connection that stands above all.

But, let's get back to the past. So, in the morning, I went to the small general store and bought an Old Hickory kitchen knife to set sail. Regarding bear defense, I consulted an old native man who told me, „You should have a long spear and carve a long, very smooth tip on it." He emphasized that the shape of the tip really mattered. Very very smooth. I asked why. „Well, if the bear sticks the pole up your ass, it won't hurt as much." With my new traditional knowledge, which meant „avoid the bear", I let the current take my boat and drifted into my greatest adventure.

The first shock was the absolute silence.

My „Bear defence pole"

DOWN WE GO

Civilization and the old life remained on the shore; flow and the vastness that can only unfold here in the North took over the day. I gripped the paddle for the first time, which would be my friend for the next two weeks. I had two, in case one caused blisters or got lost. The silence and the soundless gliding began to lull me, and from time to time, a wave of euphoria came over me, and I shouted, „I'm doing it!", reassuring myself this was really happening.

The beautiful weather I started with would soon turn into a fierce wind. And so, it became quite clear that my canoe mastery was far away from being top notch. The wind did as it pleased, and I struggled to keep the tip of my canoe pointing downstream. And then it began to rain. There was nothing left of the silent vastness and the romantic adventure. I had to go ashore, where the next lesson was waiting for me immediately. You land canoes by turning them upstream, balancing the current through paddling, and gently landing. Not by frantically sticking them downstream into a bank, flipping the canoe to the side, and thereby losing the first paddle of your journey. After dragging the rest to dry safety, I wrapped myself in my tent tarp and waited out the storm. At least I now knew for sure that the first paddle wouldn't be causing any blisters. I guarded what I still had like a hawk. The idea of whittling a second paddle never occurred to me during the whole journey, which I still find unbelievable.

The fun was almost unbearable. There I was, lying in a tent without poles, getting battered by the weather. It was actually a good time to go home, but that was over now. What mattered now was to find my strength. I needed to find what I really could do, focus on what I had learned and seen, and to hope that a solution would come to mind for every problem that arose. Finally, the stormy weather took a break, and as quickly as this lightning storm came, it was gone again. With one paddle less and a significantly better weight distribution than the first attempt, I now paddled into my first endlessly bright Yukon evening. It had begun. It was truly adventurous.

On the river

FIRST NIGHT IN THE OPEN

I chose an island for my first night because it was beautifully far away from the forest where the bears lived. That seemed safe to me. Sure, they could swim, but at least you could see them coming. The later it got, the more fear crept into my bones. Cooking noodles and drinking calming beer didn't help. I still remember the moment when I opened my diary and wrote, „I've totally overestimated myself." The circumstances I had gotten myself into exceeded my mental capacity to deal with them. With the onset of the silence of the night and my first complete aloneness, fear came. And exactly at this point, when rational thinking fails, your instincts begin to awaken.

I couldn't just get out of here. I couldn't make excuses or tell anyone „You deal with it."
I had to get myself out of here. I was the man I depended on. A big fire seemed to be the best medicine, and because I was alone for the first time, I could perform my „please don't eat me, bear" - dance with all my heart. With my beautifully smooth pointed spear, I hopped around the flames, danced with the shadows, and shouted into the forest, „Leave me alone!"

I was knee-deep in the most beautiful mess at my own request and had to save myself, literally. Fortunately, no one saw it, but who knows, maybe someone did. I scratched ration marks on the much too small whisky bottle and crawled into my tent. With wide-open ears, I layed there until the sleep of the exhausted young adventurer did me in. Nothing ate me, but in the morning, the eggs were missing. Some experienced forest creature, I thought a fox, but in hindsight, it was probably the ravens, that had my breakfast. There I stood as Yukon Robinson on my island without my eggs. At this point, it was crystal clear to me that I had to get my act together, and the only way to do that was to relax. By approaching the whole thing with calm dynamics to calm the nerves down. The river helped me with that as I drifted away that morning.

Its great tranquility began to become my friend and made more sense with every river mile. The pointless struggle against nature began to transform into observing and understanding. Slowly, very slowly.

My own island

DRIFTING INTO MYSELF

After a few days, you reach a point on the Yukon where the river definitively bids farewell to the highway. You've already been deep in the forest, but from there on, it's only river ahead. I was rather surprised when my mind actually entertained the question of giving up again and abandoning the whole thing. I didn't feel bad at all, but the unknown that lay ahead caused discomfort. I didn't want to admit it because I wanted to be a hero. But it couldn't be denied. For me, as a little 'big mouth', it became quite a big deal to navigate into the unknown, not really being sure what I was truly capable of. When everything went well, everything went well, but what if it wouldn't? What if the canoe would drift away? What if I'd break a leg or what if I was hunted? Images began to form in my mind, making any horror movie look like a soap opera. Our minds can wonderfully stand in the way of life, and I don't know why, but our „world of thought" has often absolutely nothing to do with reality.

I think our minds often prevent more than they enable, a fact that I have encountered many times in life. Again and again, I argue with myself about what is possible and what is not, about what is morally justifiable and what is just crap. But also about what one can and cannot do. And in that regard, the mind is simply insane. Of course, we can do everything we can imagine. Our ancestors did so much more with so much less, and here we are, always sitting there, collecting our problems (real and imaginary), and then simply letting go of important things. Continuing at this point was very important to me. Continuing gave me confidence. Confidence in myself. Confidence that, if no voices interfere from the inside, I could do really great things. Things that made sense to me. Things that should be lived, even if they are not on the standard menu.

And so, slowly but surely, I drifted into my new life. Little Holly on the big river in the far North. Jack London had also drifted along here and probably had ran out of coffee by now, had no return ticket and his boat was surely also crappy. So, everything was not that bad and twice as beautiful. And that's how my eyes began to open, and my mind became quieter.

I am someone who talks a lot to myself when I'm alone, so we two are never truly alone. Holly inside and Holly outside. I think this is where the love for this river began, a river that changed at every bend. The Yukon is not a postcard river, but somehow, it sure got me. Its small islands, its rock walls revealing the Earth's interior, its colors, and above all, its tranquility. It helps you when you flow with it. It continues to help me understand the world, heal me when it has hurt me, and repeatedly shows me the beauty of change.

Now, everything was going quite well, and I began to think I was „on top of the game". The load in the boat was well distributed, the food seemed to work out, and the camps I set up were improving. I had carved a pipe in the shape of a human toe from soapstone and smoked sage from the toenail. I sipped on the daily whiskey ration and practiced drifting. But, because I am Holly, one of my most unusual adventures awaited me not far ahead.

An Asian young man in Whitehorse had told me about an old man named John, with whom he had baked a pizza with 'magic mushrooms' at Coffee Creek. If I were to encounter old John, I should send regards and convey that the pizza had provided a lot of color for canoeing. Funny, I thought, and had no hope of finding the hut at the small coffee creek. Just to be on the safe side, I didn't bring a river map, and anyway, I had no idea where or how far I was. But to my surprise I found the place, and what I experienced there not only surpassed my wildest adventure expectations but also gave me a crash course in being a Yukoner. They do things a bit differently up here in the bush. So, a few parked motorboats appeared on the horizon. Something was happening, and I decided to say hello to whoever was there.

Learning how to drift

COFFEE CREEK JOHN

As I maneuvered my canoe alongside the motorboats, I noticed that these boats had worked hard.
Most of them seemed homemade, long and narrow,
equipped with quite battered propellers. Some had
fishing nets, and almost all had empty beer cans. I
crawled up the shore and found the log cabin. Well, it
wasn't much of a cabin anymore, but more like a
stack of logs, as part of the roof had already collapsed. No one was outside, but it was loud inside.
So, like in a movie, I entered a cabin in the deepest
wilderness.

Once my eyes adjusted to the darkness, I was initially
surprised at how many characters crowded into such
a small space. The place was full, and so were all the
occupants – full of moonshine, a pure alcohol called
„Everclear" here. It was immediately offered to me,
with the advice to mix it only with a mouthful of or-
ange juice – a live mix during intake. I gladly welcomed Everclear into my life, my English quickly im-
proved, and the whole crowd of bushed men
celebrated my surprise visit. Most of my new friends
were sitting at the table - because they couldn't stand
anymore. In bed, there was a young couple about to
reach their peak, and a woman stood at the kitchen
unwrapping a cake that I would soon taste. Not a
normal cake, I thought. After that first shot of moonshine, I wanted to know what was being celebrated
here. Everyone still able to lift an arm or even their
entire head pointed to the old man in the chair. He
didn't look good, but he matched the chair. Both had

been here for a while and showed signs of heavy use, with the chair still looking salvageable. So, there he was, „Coffee Creek John", and just as I was about to wish him a „possibly happy birthday", I got an elbow from the side, meaning: „If I don't have to puke right now, I'll speak in a moment."

The face next to me, resembling a topographical map with a beard, muttered, "he is dying, we drink until he's dead!" – and after a short pause he resumed – „John won't last much longer; we are almost there."

I slowly withdrew my congratulatory hand from John's direction and tried to collect myself. So, I ended up at a party in the middle of nowhere where there would be a dead person in the end? I looked at John. The recently made statement didn't seem to bother him, prompting me to check if he was even still moving. John sat slouched in his chair nest, coughed heavily at times, breathing shallowly, and only woke up when a fresh bottle of Everclear was opened. I had never been so close to someone who was at „The End" and my journey took a rather mystical turn in the old trapper's cabin.

The figures, whom I probably all know personally today, as long as they're still alive, all looked like characters from old movies, only more real. They were the old film; I was now right in the middle of one. The missing roof was covered with a tarp that directed rainwater directly into the bathtub in the room. Old shoes, traps, furs, and lots of utilities for the great outdoors hung on the walls. The young couple on the bed was breathing faster and I reached for the bottle. Strangely, I thought they would have it all under control, and I would just observe. There was a lot of laughter, adventurous stories were told, of which I understood only half, and John stayed alive. To my surprise, late at night, the first Yukoners started staggering to their boats and disappeared into the wilderness. It was funny at first, until I was left with only John and a woman. The woman then handed me a walkie talkie and explained that she was leaving too, and I should radio her if John dies. My eyes widened, and I said in clear German-English, „Noooooo!". My fear of being left alone with the old man was so evident that she just laughed and let me go. I also staggered to my canoe, layed down, and drifted away. Paddling was barely possible. Eventually, I found a spot where even a drunkard could be beached. I crawled as far as I could and wrapped myself in my sleeping bag and fell asleep. John died a few days later. I don't know why I didn't stay. In hindsight, I might have been able to stay, but the whole scene was still a bit too adventurous for little Holly. The next day, as I drifted down the river with a headache for two, I thought for the first time in plain English:

„What the fuck just happened?"

Coffee Creek John's Cabin

AGAINST THE WIND

Just before the White River joins in from the left,
turning the Yukon into glacier milk, I encountered
my next stumbling block. Headwind, and a strong
one, was blown directly upstream. So strong that I
couldn't make any progress down the river. Every
time I tried to turn around the bend, the storm
pushed me back. And being German, waiting for the
weather to change is for wimps. Instead, you prefer
to paddle in place for a day. The moose probably
rolled on the ground laughing as the same idiot
passed by ten times in both directions.

Only when I was almost at my wit's end did the wisdom box snap open. Loading the canoe with rocks
was the key. With a heavy ship, the current carries
you through. Many years later, an old-timer taught
me that in such a case, you drag a tree with many
branches into the water and tie the canoe to it. The
tree pulls you, and you can enjoy a coffee. I had already learned to cook in the boat, only the stove
shouldn't tip over. When you spend so much time in
a canoe, you learn a lot, but I wish I had known
about the tree trick earlier.

However, one was delighted when one had survived
such a shit show. It wasn't until later in life that I realized that during an adventure, things are usually terribly exhausting, and you can hardly appreciate the
beauty of the moment. Somehow, though, our sub-
consciousness manages to secretly record all those
moments and later presents them to us as memories
and stories. Even now, as I write this (over 20 years

later), I feel like I'm in that boat. Images and emotions appear as if it's happening right now. I can even feel the old striped sweater and the wind again.

I knew that after the confluence of the White River and the Yukon, a small settlement would appear on the right. An old trading post, where the Steward River flows in. The woman in Coffee Creek John's cabin had told me that her family had lived there forever. Finally, I had a navigation point to cling on to. When I'd see the cabins, I'd still be two days away from Dawson, and today they should appear. You'd think that because a river has a shore on both sides, a watchful adventurer wouldn't miss anything. But no matter how far I paddled – no settlement. This raised two thoughts in me that didn't contribute to my reassurance. Either the way was much longer than I thought, making my supplies and whiskey bottle look quite meager. Or I simply had missed it. But then again, this would mean I could also miss Dawson? How big was it? Was it behind an island? What if I'd already passed it? Great. Not much is coming after Dawson down there, and I started to get pretty uneasy. I could have prepared a bit better by bringing a map. But I still don't do that today, and that's why I always have to work with a bit of uncertainty. This was another one of those moments. Two days after the settlement I was supposed to find, I was paddling in the „grand river of time" and had no idea whether the next person I'd see would speak Russian or if I would find myself as a very thin pirate in the Bering Sea in two months. A shitty feeling, I can tell you. If I had had a phone-joker option, I would have used it.

My rescue came in the form of two flower power children. The hippie couple had set up camp on a small island with their canoe and were the first people I had seen in a long time. They seemed to have a Zen attitude and enjoyed their little island paradise. When I learned from them that I was already very close to Dawson, my inner sun came out again. Relieved that I wouldn't be found as a skeleton, and the fact that my river journey was almost over, led directly to a sip from the whiskey bottle. I left one in there for Dawson.

The hours I spent on their island with them and the night in my last camp before Dawson were finally lived in bliss. The uncertainty gone, and the good feeling of having done it alone made my eyes and heart open wide. There it was, the Yukon, and somehow, I felt like I had become a small part of it. For a while, I had lived a completely different life in an unknown place. I had been a hundred percent the master of my time and the sole owner of my mistakes. I was the captain, but had to do everything myself. I was free. Not that I was very unfree before, but it looked like I had my hand back on the wheel of my own ship. This brought more responsibility, but I felt more balanced. Unconsciously, the feeling arose that changes of direction were allowed again. What I didn't know yet was that this small, quirky, wild, and unpredictably tough city ahead of me would once again completely turn my life upside down. I was still standing in the river mud with my shoes, unaware that I was about to enter a world that I thought had disappeared in the past. A world where many spirits have remained, and where I would also get caught in the net of its charm. On the last miles before Dawson, I was still a wanderer and a wonderer. But soon, I would come home, come home to a world so unfamiliar and yet so familiar: Dawson fucking City.

The last night out there

DAWSON CITY, THE END OF THIS ROAD

When I first saw the colorful houses on the right side
of the river, I was super glad that I hadn't missed
them. You know, just taking a little canoe nap and
drifting right past them. No, I was wide awake, ready
to embrace the Paris of the North. But to do that, I
had to paddle like crazy to get to the other side. The
Klondike flows in from the right and pushes you
nicely to the other side. And the Yukon gets pretty
fast here too. But the ambition of an East German
athlete helped me switch sides, and so I moored my
beautiful yellow canoe at the boat dock next to an
airplane and squeezed the last drop of whiskey from
the flask. Everything hurt, and I was hungry to see
people. I'd had enough of talking to myself, explaining how the world works only to not believe it myself. And so, there I sat, legs in the boat, proud to
have done all this, gazing into the sun when the first
representative of the „Dawsonites" appeared. His
name was Mo. Mo was tall, a Rasta type, and the first
words I ever heard in Dawson came from him.
„Beer?" - „Yes, Sir" - I said, after which he asked me
to follow him.

Mo took me to the Pit. My canoe stayed with all my
stuff simply at the dock. No stealing in Paradise. I
strolled with Mo past a historic paddlewheeler, wandered through a set of houses that seemed to have
fallen out of the last John Wayne film, and ended up
in front of an old hotel. A hotel that was painted in a
very obvious color choice… pink. And as it turned
out, that was the most ordinary thing about this

house. It was already night, but, of course, rather bright up here in the North when I opened the door to the Westminster Hotel and stepped into its romantic darkness.

In the lobby, there was a mammoth skull at the reception. Nobody had been received here for a long time, and as I passed through the second door, the first warm wave of comfort grabbed me. Packed to the rafters, this bar wasn't just a bar. Rather a ship, full of fools, pirates, princesses, and a lot of dubious characters. On stage, a band that didn't look so good anymore but played as if this was their „Last Day". And then there was smoke, a lot of smoke. When the first beer hit me like I slipped off the clutch, my world became colorful. After all the black-and-white thinking that life had trained me for, I landed right in the rainbow of a society unknown to me. Like a young fish, I immediately began to revel in it and let all the good things run over my delightfully tipsy mind. Mo introduced me to two loud and very, very funny French Canadians. The hippie girls immediately invited me to stay with them in their treehouse. I graciously accepted and ordered more beer. It was one of the most glorious moments of my life to arrive in a place that seemed to have been waiting for me. Every person looked interesting; not a single ordinary person was present. Every song made you listen, and people danced as if no one was watching. Some even danced lying down. I was blissful. Finally, a wild horde that seemed to know no rules.

After way too much of a good thing, I staggered early in the morning to the canoe and sailed to the other side, where the ladies welcomed me, and they led me to the treehouse. It was high and cute and gave me the sleep that an adventurer dreams about. Warm and cuddly and intoxicated. Goodnight Dawson... I already love you.

I wanted to stay here for three days but after thirteen, I was still living in the treehouse. Mo had disappeared into the bush with another friend. The guests changed constantly, and every evening, we met at the Pit to evaluate the days and celebrate the nights. I felt like I was 16 again and could hardly get enough of looking at the people I encountered. They were all so much funnier than the naysayers. I had the impression of not only encountering a new society but also a new way of thinking. Fun came first, not the problem. Inside of me, naturally, was still a rock-solid German core holding its ground, but my emotions and feelings had already mingled with the rainbow people. Until today, I prefer to surround myself with this tribe, carrying a cheerfulness within them and showing it gladly, existing in every country of the world. I'm not always happy, but I've learned from them that it's possible to approach life differently. You can get the stick out of your ass. You can run into life without constantly disciplining yourself. They were good people who welcomed me in Dawson, and I wanted to be a good person from now on. With all the courage for change, with all the stories and people who led me here, and with the fortune of the seeker, I had actually arrived at my own transformation.

I had arrived at the end of the road to begin to reinvent myself. And then...

Well, that's enough for a whole new book.

Arrival in Dawson City

HOW LIFE GOES SOMETIMES...

I would like to make you, dear reader, some appetite for more of my stories and at the same time encourage you to go play with your own life.

Then ... something nice can happen to you.

I had promised one more story from the master of grunge rock, Neil Young.

So, let's go.

At some point I was watching a concert by the hero of my youth on YouTube, when I noticed that Neil had created a wonderful living room atmosphere on stage with a lot of love. Everything looked very cozy, except for the awful microphone stands sticking out of the carpet like water pipes. The things completely destroyed the whole picture for me as a hardcore romantic and I decided to tackle this problem.

The next day's found me in the Yukon Forest hunting for diamond willows. A precious wood that is not only unbreakable, but looks fantastic when you have fumbled the bark off. Then I dragged the selected branches into the workshop and conjured up a combination from conventional mic stands and the noble wood. It looked stunning.

But the problem was that I didn't know Neil personally and so I offered it to life itself, how the beautiful thing should make it to Young.

A while later (in my time maybe even two years), we set off to cross the whole of Canada with a school bus powered by used vegetable oil, two children in permanent headstand and our dog. I thought I'd take the microphone stand with me; you never know who you run into. Kinda, keep your eyes open and hope. When we were, during this trip on Salt Spring Island / British Columbia, it dawned on me that Randy Bachman, singer of „The Guess Who" and lifelong friend of Neil Young, also lives on this island and it didn't take long until I rang his doorbell. But he didn't answer because he wasn't there.

Shit, I thought that was close. I sat down in a coffee shop with my Neil biography „Waging Heavy Peace", which I was reading at the time and was sad. After a short coffee enjoyment, someone approached me about the book and I immediately poured all my suffering over this person, that I can never bring my work of art to Neil and the world therefore looks quite terrible. The good man then smiled pitifully and asked if I knew a man named Daryl. He is a music producer and studio owner on the island, knows Randy and maybe Daryl can do something. My eyes lit up a bit and not too much later my thumb pressed the doorbell right next to the sign „Please do not disturb" of the Recording Studio. The door opened and a young man with an Albert Einstein~hairdo stares at me incomprehensibly.

Hello, I'm Holly and I have a mic stand for Neil Young. Daryl stood there in awe, then gathered himself and grinned, after shaking his head. I didn't know if he thought „This is soo weird" or if he was just laughing at me. The grin became greater and two wild souls recognized each other. „Come on in, that's incredible!" I entered in amazement a wonderful music studio right on the beach of the Pacific, where a lot of history had already taken place and my new friend said

„Well, put that thing up". After a satisfied assessment and an even wider grin, he asked me to sit down and began his presentation.

„So look…yesterday, yes yesterday, I signed the contract to be stage manager on the next "Neil Young and Crazy Horse" tour. The first paragraph of the contract states that it is strictly forbidden to bring any fan gifts for Neil and everyone else. But this thing is soo cool, we will try it!"

I think I cried a bit with joy and would have been very satisfied with just this outcome. Of course, Daryl couldn't promise anything, but I knew he would risk it, if a moment came up that seemed appropriate. I handed over the work for my hero and we separated in friendship with the words „That might take a while", which means „don't push".

When this Crazy Horse Tour actually took place many moons later, the travel life had already washed us to Mexico. We were residing in a youth hostel in Sayulita when an email came from Daryl that didn't say much more than „call me".

When the connection was finally established between Mexico and Canada, I was listening to Daryl's heart-warming and very moving story that my Neil Young was so happy to get such a fine Yukon~work of art that he will bring it to his music barn, that he now knows who I am and thanks me very much, that he was very impressed that we brought our children to school with the dog sled and that he wishes me good luck with my music.

When I dropped the receiver into the fork afterwards, this warm honey feeling came over me, which pours itself exclusively after cheeky, pushed by enthusiasm, crazy adventures over me, when they have a happy ending like this.

I live for this kind of thing. These moments make it always worth it for me to go the extra mile and these stories are then the reward of my imagination. I love the impossible, because it can be so surprisingly fresh. I just like to dream big.

See you at the next limit of what is possible, and then step over it.

Your's truly

Driftwood Holly

Foto von Sara Katharina Müller

Fire~Tour 2024 (Germany)

LAFEYA

Out on your into the wild
You way home with a crooked smile
I will not die until the day
Our little love has come to stay

I look right through you when you disappear
Coming in to out of here
I will not lie until the end
When all the truth will settle in

Deida deida dumm...

You just hold me to let go
I´ll tell you everything that I don`t know

So let`s get up we`re coming down
Our masterpiece our little town
So I get up I`m falling free
My masterpiece can stay with thee

Deida deida dumm...

I look right through you when you disappear
Coming in to out of here
I will not lie until the end
When all the truth will settle in

From the album „Aura Borealis"

Here is space for your dreams an wises. Write them down before you put it back on the shelf an come back later to revisit. Thank you...